DELICIOUS
VEGETARIAN COOKING

BY

IVAN BAKER

Dover Publications, Inc.
New York

This Dover edition, first published in 1972, is an unabridged republication of the work originally published in 1954 by G. Bell & Sons, Ltd., under the title *Complete Vegetarian Recipe Book*. It is reprinted by special arrangement with G. Bell & Sons, Ltd., York House, Portugal Street, London W.C.2, England.

International Standard Book Number: 0-486-22834-7
Library of Congress Catalog Card Number: 72-189775

Manufactured in the United States of America
Dover Publications, Inc.
180 Varick Street
New York, N.Y. 10014

PREFACE

VEGETARIAN diet excludes all fish, flesh, and fowl. Every other kind of food is used in the preparation of vegetarian dishes. Various cheeses, eggs, butter, milk, cereals, vegetables, nuts, pulses, salad materials, fruits, vegetable fats, oils and sugars, are therefore among the ingredients of the recipes numbering over 475 in this book.

If a dinner is to begin with hors d'œuvre or soup, followed by a main dish with a suitable sauce and vegetable garnish, the necessary items can be quickly chosen after a glance at the relevant chapters. There are light savouries, salads, sweet dishes including popular puddings, pies, pastries, and other desserts for the completion of menus and for occasional use.

Topical interest in the bread we eat has not been overlooked. Recipes for home made bread and other foods made of real whole wheat flour are included.

The recipes are presented so as to bring out basic cookery methods, and if this intention has been achieved, the reader with a rudimentary experience of cooking may learn the essentials by simply trying out the recipes. For the experienced cook, following the recipes will be plain sailing. In either case, the dishes will be tasty and attractive, provided that good quality ingredients are used.

Meals will be amply nutritious if they include one of the many main dishes. Their 'food values', though not discussed, are a vitally important part of the recipes.

I. B.

LONDON,
April 1954

CONVERSION TABLES FOR FOREIGN EQUIVALENTS

DRY INGREDIENTS

Ounces		Grams	Grams		Ounces	Pounds		Kilograms	Kilograms		Pounds
1	=	28.35	1	=	0.035	1	=	0.454	1	=	2.205
2		56.70	2		0.07	2		0.91	2		4.41
3		85.05	3		0.11	3		1.36	3		6.61
4		113.40	4		0.14	4		1.81	4		8.82
5		141.75	5		0.18	5		2.27	5		11.02
6		170.10	6		0.21	6		2.72	6		13.23
7		198.45	7		0.25	7		3.18	7		15.43
8		226.80	8		0.28	8		3.63	8		17.64
9		255.15	9		0.32	9		4.08	9		19.84
10		283.50	10		0.35	10		4.54	10		22.05
11		311.85	11		0.39	11		4.99	11		24.26
12		340.20	12		0.42	12		5.44	12		26.46
13		368.55	13		0.46	13		5.90	13		28.67
14		396.90	14		0.49	14		6.35	14		30.87
15		425.25	15		0.53	15		6.81	15		33.08
16		453.60	16		0.57						

LIQUID INGREDIENTS

Liquid Ounces		Milliliters	Milliliters		Liquid Ounces	Quarts		Liters	Liters		Quarts
1	=	29.573	1	=	0.034	1	=	0.946	1	=	1.057
2		59.15	2		0.07	2		1.89	2		2.11
3		88.72	3		0.10	3		2.84	3		3.17
4		118.30	4		0.14	4		3.79	4		4.23
5		147.87	5		0.17	5		4.73	5		5.28
6		177.44	6		0.20	6		5.68	6		6.34
7		207.02	7		0.24	7		6.62	7		7.40
8		236.59	8		0.27	8		7.57	8		8.45
9		266.16	9		0.30	9		8.52	9		9.51
10		295.73	10		0.33	10		9.47	10		10.57

Gallons (American)		Liters	Liters		Gallons (American)
1	=	3.785	1	=	0.264
2		7.57	2		0.53
3		11.36	3		0.79
4		15.14	4		1.06
5		18.93	5		1.32
6		22.71	6		1.59
7		26.50	7		1.85
8		30.28	8		2.11
9		34.07	9		2.38
10		37.86	10		2.74

Publisher's Note to the American Edition

Both the liquid and dry measures of capacity used in this book are British imperial measures. The liquid measures are a little more than 20% larger than the corresponding American ones; one British imperial gallon, for example, is approximately equivalent to five American quarts. The difference between British and American dry measures—pint, quart, etc.—is only 5% and may be disregarded for most of the recipes in this book. However, baked goods such as cakes, pastries and biscuits may require shorter cooking times (and the number of eggs should be decreased by approximately one-fourth if the recipe uses three or more eggs). All measures of weight—pounds, ounces, etc.—used in this book are the same as those used in the United States.

Some of the ingredients called for in recipes may be unfamiliar to the average American cook. Such things as yeast extract, red lentils, agar, custard powder, angelica can be obtained in gourmet food stores, health shops, or oriental or Near Eastern groceries. While some of the vegetables can only be obtained in England, American substitutes will provide good results. The following list indicates some possible substitutions and also the common American designation for certain ingredients.

British ingredient	American ingredient
haricot beans	string beans
swede	yellow turnips, rutabaga
vegetable marrow	zucchini or pattypan squash
treacle	molasses
pine kernels	pinola nuts
golden syrup	Karo syrup
butter beans	large lima beans
field mushrooms	ordinary commercial mushrooms
aubergines	eggplant

CONTENTS

*The recipes provide sufficient for 4 to 6
persons except where otherwise stated*

SOUPS

French Onion Soup

3 lb. onions	2 well toasted rolls
1 clove garlic	1 teaspoon salt
1 bouquet garni*	pinch each : sugar and nutmeg
4 oz. butter	1 quart water

Chop the onions, mince the garlic, put in the soup pan with the herbs, butter, seasoning and a cup of hot water. Cover with a close fitting lid, cook very gently 3½ hours. Add 1 quart water and simmer ½ hour. Put the toasted rolls in the tureen, pour the soup in just before serving. Grated cheese is good with it.

Cereal Soup

1 heaped tablespoon each:	1 oz. butter
barley, rice, coarse oatmeal,	¼ lb. mushrooms
lentils	2 bay leaves
2 oz. macaroni	seasoning
½ lb. onions	3 pints water

Wash barley, rice, oatmeal and red lentils, soak in cold water ½ hour. Put chopped onions, sliced mushrooms, bay leaves, butter and seasoning in the soup pan, cover, cook gently 15 minutes, shaking pan from time to time. Add the hot water and soaked cereals, simmer ½ hour, boil up, skim, add broken macaroni, simmer 1 hour more.

Cauliflower Cream Soup

1 large cauliflower	yolk of 1 egg
1½ pints milk	¼ cup cream
½ pint white sauce	pinch each: salt and pepper

Trim the leaves and midribs from the cauliflower, divide into sprigs, cover with cold water, boil till very tender. Drain, pass through

---

* Always remove the *Bouquet Garni* (the bunch of parsley, thyme and bay leaf used for flavourings) before serving the soup.

sieve, return puree to a rinsed pan, stir in the sauce. Gradually stir in the hot milk. Beat the yolk of the egg, blend with a cup of the cooled soup, then stir into the rest of the soup. Reheat very gently without boiling. Just before serving, correct seasoning, and stir in the cream. Serve with grated cheese, toasted rolls and butter pats.

Russian Beet Soup

6 oz. cooked beet	½ pint white sauce
1 herb bouquet	¼ pint sour cream
1 small onion	1 teaspoon sugar
½ lemon	pinch each: salt and nutmeg
1 quart water	

Grate the cooked beet and the raw onion, and put them in the soup pan with the herbs, seasonings and water. Simmer 20 minutes, pass through sieve and return to a fresh pan. Stir in the white sauce, simmer 5 minutes. Add the juice of the ½ lemon. Reheat gently. Off the heat, stir in the sour cream. Serve hot with mashed potatoes, dark rye bread and butter pats. The soup is also served cold, very cold, garnished with a blob of whipped cream, and still with hot mashed potatoes. *Note 1.* When cream is absent, stir the juice of ½ lemon into ¼ pint unsweetened evaporated milk, and use as directed.   *2.* The yolk of an egg is sometimes added to the finished soup, or, indeed, the yolks of 2 eggs. (See Cauliflower Cream Soup, above.)

Mushroom Noodle Soup

½ lb. mushrooms	1 clove garlic
¼ lb. noodles	3 pints water
1 cup cooked peas	1 teaspoon yeast extract
½ oz. butter	seasoning
6 oz. onions	

Slice the mushrooms and onions, put in the soup pan with the butter, seasoning, grated garlic and half a cup of the water. Cover, and simmer 15 minutes, shaking pan now and then. Add the rest of the water, bring to the boil, throw in the noodles, simmer ½ hour. Add the cooked peas, stir in the extract, simmer 10 minutes more. Serve hot. *Note.* Spinach noodles, i.e. narrow ribbon macaroni containing spinach may be used for variation. (See Spinach Noodle Pie, p. 57.)

Vermicelli Soup

3 oz. vermicelli
1 cup fried onions
3 pints vegetable stock

1 teaspoon yeast extract
seasoning

Sprinkle broken vermicelli into the boiling stock, add fried onions, extract and seasoning, simmer ½ hour. Serve hot with grated cheese.

Clear Consommé

½ lb. haricot beans
1 oz. mushrooms
2 large onions
1 carrot
2 stalks celery

1 herb bouquet
2 teaspoons yeast extract
seasoning
2 quarts water

Wash the beans, cut up the vegetables, put all the ingredients in the soup pan, simmer 3 hours. Strain through fine cloth, then strain again, adjust the seasoning. Add any preferred garnish to each portion, e.g. a slice of hard boiled egg, a tiny dumpling, a spoonful of peas, or a cube of savoury rice. *Note.* To prepare Savoury Rice, boil 2 tablespoons rice, drain, stir in grated cheese, onion, and seasoning to taste, stand till firm, cut into cubes.

Pumpkin Cream Soup

1 lb. peeled pumpkin
¼ lb. onions
1 heart celery
½ pint white sauce

2 bay leaves
pinch each: salt and nutmeg
1 quart water

Cut the pumpkin into chunks, chop onions, slice celery and turn all into the soup pan. Add seasonings, bay leaves and water. Boil up, simmer 1 hour, pass through sieve, return the purée to a rinsed pan, add the white sauce and reheat gently till piping hot. *Note.* Vegetable marrow, or custard marrow may be prepared in the same way as the pumpkin in this recipe.

Butter Bean and Vegetable Soup

2 cups cooked butter beans
2 large onions
1 carrot
1 bouquet garni

1 teaspoon yeast extract
salt, pepper and nutmeg
3 pints water

Slice onions, cut carrot into very tiny dice, put both in the pan, add herbs, extract and water. Simmer 1 hour. Remove herbs. Add the cooked beans, pepper and nutmeg, simmer ½ hour more. Add only a pinch of salt at the end, if considered necessary as the extract probably contains sufficient salt for this soup.

Julienne Soup

1 heart celery	4 oz. onions
2 leeks	1 herb bouquet
2 carrots	1 teaspoon yeast extract
4 oz. mushrooms	3 pints water
1 oz. butter	seasoning

Cut the prepared vegetables into fine shreds, put them in the soup pan with the butter, herbs, seasoning and water. Cover pan tightly, simmer gently 15 minutes, shaking pan occasionally. Add water, bring to boil, simmer 1 hour or until the vegetables are quite tender. Remove herbs, stir in extract. Serve hot.

Leek Broth with Cheese

4 thick leeks	1 teaspoon salt
½ lb. potatoes	dash of pepper
1 onion	2 quarts water
1 oz. rice	grated cheese
1 oz butter	

Thinly slice the trimmed leeks and onion, stew gently with the butter for 10 minutes. Add the thinly sliced potatoes, seasonings and hot water. Cook gently 15 minutes. Add the rice and cook 45 minutes more. Sprinkle a spoonful of grated cheese into each portion when serving.

Tomato Cream Soup (using tomato juice)

2 cups tinned tomato juice	½ cup cream
1 tablespoon butter	pinch each: pepper, salt, sugar,
½ oz. flour	nutmeg
½ pint milk	

Melt the butter in a saucepan, stir in the flour, cook and stir, without browning, for 2 minutes. Gradually stir in milk, simmer 5 minutes.

Add the seasonings, then gradually stir in the tomato juice. Cook very gently, without boiling, until thoroughly hot. Off the heat, stir in the cream. Serve hot. *Note*. Taste for seasoning before serving, so that correction may be made if desired.

Potato Purée

2 lb. potatoes	1½ pints thin white sauce
1 onion	½ oz. butter (see p. 21)
mint or parsley	seasoning

Boil the potatoes and onion with a pinch of seasoning, drain, save cooking water, mash smooth with the butter. Stir in the sauce and cooking water. Heat gently until hot. Garnish each portion with shredded mint or parsley.

Vegetable Barley Broth

4 oz. each: carrot, onion, celery	1 teaspoon yeast extract
2 oz. barley	2 quarts water
1 herb bouquet	seasoning
1 oz. butter	

Soak the washed barley 15 minutes. Dice the vegetables and put in the soup pan with the butter, herbs, seasoning, and a cup of the water. Cover, cook gently 15 minutes, shaking the pan now and then. Add soaked barley and the rest of the water, and simmer 1½ hours. Stir in extract and simmer 5 minutes more.

Cabbage Soup with Rice

1 lb. cabbage	1 teaspoon salt
½ lb. onions	dash pepper and nutmeg
2 oz. rice	1 teaspoon yeast extract
1 herb bouquet	2 quarts water
1 oz. butter	½ cup cream

Shred cabbage coarsely, slice onions, put both in the soup pan with the butter, herbs, seasoning and a cup of water. Cover, and simmer 15 minutes, shaking pan from time to time. Add water, yeast extract and rice, and simmer 1½ hours. Just before serving, stir in the cream.

Thick Vegetable Soup (1)

3 oz. each: sliced runner beans,   1 oz. butter
   diced carrot, diced potato,   1 oz. vermicelli
   sliced mushrooms, sliced   1 herb bouquet
   celery, sliced peeled tomatoes   1 teaspoon yeast extract
4 oz. onions   seasoning
1 oz. red lentils   2 quarts water

Lightly brown the sliced onions in the butter, add all the remaining ingredients, bring slowly to the boil, simmer 1½ hours. Remove herb bouquet. Serve hot.

Thick Vegetable Soup (2)

2 oz. each: cabbage, carrot,   2 oz. margarine
   turnip   1 clove garlic
4 oz. potato   seasoning
1 tablespoon each: barley, red   2 quarts water
   lentils, broken macaroni   1 teaspoon yeast extract
1 lb. onions

Slowly fry the sliced onions and garlic in the margarine till lightly coloured, then turn them into the soup pan. Add the shredded cabbage, shredded carrot, diced turnip and potato, the cereals, seasoning and water. Boil up, skim, simmer 2 hours. Stir in extract. Serve hot. *Note.* The slow frying of the onions makes the soup delicious. Butter instead of margarine is an improvement.

Barley Cream Soup

3 oz. each: carrot, turnip,   1 tablespoon barley
   swede   1 tablespoon flour
1 leek (white part)   ½ cup milk or cream
yolk of 1 egg   1 teaspoon butter
seasoning   1 quart water

Grate the root vegetables into the soup pan. Slice the leek and add. Add barley, seasoning and water. Boil up, skim, simmer 1 hour. Make a paste of the flour and a little cold water and add. Simmer 1 hour more. Blend beaten yolk with the milk or cream and add. Reheat the soup gently but it must not boil. Stir in the butter just before serving. *Note.* When obtainable, use barley flour instead of flour.

Potato Cheese Purée

1 lb. mashed potatoes	½ pint evaporated milk
1 grated onion	1½ pints water
3 oz. grated cheese	3 oz. grated cheese
½ oz. butter	seasoning

Put mashed potato, onion, butter and seasoning in the soup pan, stir over gentle heat for 3 minutes. Moisten with the hot water, simmer 10 minutes. Stir in the evaporated milk and make hot without boiling. Off the heat, stir in the grated cheese and serve without delay.

Vegetable Chowder

¼ lb. each: diced celery and carrot	1 quart milk
	1½ oz. butter
½ lb. onions	1 tablespoon parsley
½ lb. potatoes	1 teaspoon salt
1 cup cooked peas	pepper and nutmeg
¼ pint water	

Melt the butter in the soup pan, add the diced celery and carrot, sliced onions and potatoes, seasoning and water. Cover pan and stew gently 15 minutes shaking pan occasionally. Add half the milk and simmer gently 1 hour. Add the rest of the milk and the chopped parsley, simmer 10 minutes more.

Potato Cream Soup

1 lb. potatoes	½ cup cream or evaporated milk
1 onion	1 herb bouquet
½ oz. butter	seasoning
1 quart water	

Simmer the potatoes, sliced onion, herbs and seasoning in the water for ½ hour then rub through the soup sieve. Reheat the purée gently, stir in butter and cream. Serve hot.

Green Pea Purée

1 tin garden peas	4 sprigs mint
1 cup cooked mixed vegetables	½ oz. butter
1 grated raw onion	seasoning
1 quart water	

Put all the ingredients, except butter, in the soup pan, simmer 10 minutes, pass through strainer or sieve, reheat, stir in butter, correct seasoning. Serve hot.

Green Lentil and Tomato Broth

½ lb. green lentils	1 herb bouquet
½ lb. tomatoes	3 cloves
½ lb. onions	3 pints water
1 oz. butter	seasoning

Soak the lentils 8 hours. Chop the onions and brown in the butter. Peel and chop tomatoes and put in the soup pan. Add lentils, onions, herbs, cloves and seasoning. Moisten with the water. Simmer 2 hours, correct seasoning. Serve hot.

Minestrone

1 cup each: sliced celery, small dice of carrot, swede, and potatoes	1 cup cooked peas
	1 oz. butter
	1 herb bouquet
½ lb. onions	seasoning
1 clove garlic	2 quarts water
2 oz. vermicelli	

Slice the onions, mince garlic fine, brown both in the butter and put in the soup pan. Add the other vegetables, herbs, seasoning and water. Boil up, skim, simmer 1 hour. Add the broken vermicelli and simmer 15 minutes. Add the cooked peas and simmer 15 minutes more. Remove herb bouquet. Serve hot.

Mushroom and Vegetable Soup

3 pints vegetable stock	4 oz. fried mushrooms
3 oz. semolina	2 bay leaves
1 cup diced cooked vegetables	seasoning
1 cup cooked peas	

Sprinkle semolina into the boiling stock and stir 5 minutes while the stock simmers. Add the vegetables, mushrooms, peas, bay leaves and seasoning. Simmer 10 minutes. Remove bay leaves. Serve with grated cheese.

Tomato Soup with Rice

½ lb. tomatoes	2 oz. rice
2 onions	1 quart water
1 herb bouquet	½ teaspoon salt
1 oz. butter	pinch each: pepper and nutmeg

Chop the onions, brown slightly in the butter, add the sliced peeled tomatoes, the washed rice, water and seasonings. Simmer 1 hour. Remove herbs. Serve hot.

Lentil Cream Soup

½ lb. red lentils	1 quart milk
1 herb bouquet	1 teaspoon yeast extract
2 onions	seasoning
1 pint white sauce	

Wash the lentils, put in the soup pan with the sliced onions, herbs, seasonings and water to cover. Simmer ½ hour, pass through sieve, strainer or soup mill. Add white sauce and milk. Simmer 15 minutes. Stir in extract just before serving.

Buckwheat and Potato Soup

1 lb. potatoes	1 cup evaporated milk
½ lb. onions	1 herb bouquet
3 oz. buckwheat (kasha)	seasoning
3 pints water	

Cut the potatoes into sections, slice the onions, put both in the soup pan with the herbs, seasoning, buckwheat and water. Boil up, skim, simmer 1 hour. Stir in the evaporated milk (unsweetened), simmer gently till hot, remove herbs. *Note.* ' Kasha ' is slightly roasted buckwheat, and is sold by most Continental stores. If not obtainable, replace by the same amount of coarse oatmeal.

Vegetable Stock

2 lb. (total) outer leaves of cabbage, outer celery stalks, green part of leeks	2 herb bouquets
	2 quarts water
	6 peppercorns
carrots	1 teaspoon salt
onions	1 teaspoon yeast extract
1 oz. red lentils	

Cleanse and cut up the vegetables, wash the lentils, put in the soup pan with the remaining ingredients. Boil gently 1 hour. Strain off the liquid. Use as directed. *Note.* Beans of various kinds, even when too old for serving as such, are valuable for stock making. Add, when available, to the rest of the stock ingredients, and increase water.

Tomato Soup

½ lb. tomatoes
1 oz. butter
1 herb bouquet
1 small onion stuck with 4 cloves

1 quart vegetable stock or vegetable cooking water
½ pint white sauce
1 teaspoon each salt and sugar
pinch each: pepper and nutmeg

Stew the peeled tomatoes in butter till soft. Add the onion, herbs, stock, seasonings and spices. Simmer 20 minutes, pass through sieve or fine strainer, return to a rinsed pan, add white sauce, simmer gently without boiling till thoroughly hot. *Note.* When ripe tomatoes are not available, bottled, canned, or frosted tomatoes, or concentrated tomato purée may replace them with satisfactory results.

Vegetable Marrow Soup

1 lb. vegetable marrow
4 oz. onion
1 herb bouquet
1 oz. butter

1 quart milk
½ oz. flour
1 teaspoon salt
pinch each: pepper and nutmeg

Cut up the marrow and onion, put in the soup pan with the herbs and seasonings, cover with water, boil gently ½ hour. Pass through sieve, return to rinsed pan; make paste of the flour, butter and a spoonful of the soup, and add. Add the milk. Simmer gently 15 minutes with seasoning to taste.

SOUP GARNISHES

Almond Dumplings

½ oz. ground almonds	1 tablespoon milk
1½ oz. bread crumbs	¾ oz. butter
1 egg	seasoning

Pour the milk on half the bread crumbs. Cream the butter, add the soaked bread crumbs, ground almonds, seasonings, the rest of the crumbs and the slightly beaten egg. Form into light, walnut size balls, using a few more dry bread crumbs if necessary. Drop them into boiling water or soup, cover pan, simmer 5 minutes.

Omelet Noodles

Mix 2 tablespoons cooked noodles with 1 beaten egg and a pinch of seasoning. Cook as an omelet, roll up tightly when done, press between 2 plates for a few minutes. Slice the roll and add to hot soup just before serving.

Sponge Balls

1 egg	2 tablespoons flour
1 dessertspoon butter	pinch each: salt and nutmeg

Cream the butter light, stir in the beaten egg. Gradually beat in the flour, add seasoning. With floured hands, shape the mixture into marbles. Drop into boiling soup. They take 3 minutes to cook. *Note.* These may be prepared in advance for use as required. They are nice cold, as a salad garnish. They can be re-heated in simmering soup or stock.

Soup Noisettes

4 oz. stale bread crumbs	1 tablespoon milk
1 level tablespoon butter	pinch minced parsley
1 small egg	pinch dried thyme
½ cup mashed potato	pinch each: salt and pepper

Heat the milk and pour on half the bread crumbs, mix well with the potato, butter, herbs and seasonings, and the rest of the bread

19

crumbs. Add the beaten egg gradually, as a rather firm dough is required, and all the egg may not be necessary. Shape into walnut size balls, roll in flour, drop into boiling soup or stew, after which, reduce heat and simmer 3 minutes.

Cheese Risolettes

Add a tablespoon of grated cheese to the mixture for Soup Noisettes (see p. 19), shape into florin size rissoles, coat in beaten egg, fry in hot butter Use as a garnish for soups, stews and savouries.

Saffron Rice Squares

3 oz. rice
6 shreds saffron *
1 slice onion

1 egg
pinch each: salt and nutmeg

Boil the rice with the saffron and onion until very tender, drain, add beaten egg and seasonings, spread ½ inch deep in a buttered fireproof dish. Bake gently till dry and firm, and when quite cold cut into 1-inch squares. Add to hot soup or stew just before serving.

Shredded Bread

Shred a thick slice of stale wholemeal bread, put the shreds on a lightly greased tin and bake slowly until dry and crisp. Add to clear or thin soups when serving.

Soup Croutons

Cut stale bread into small, neat cubes. Toss in a little butter for 3 minutes. Add to soups when serving.

Duchess Dumplings

1 lb. mashed potatoes
1 egg
2 oz. flour

pinch each: salt and nutmeg
small bread cubes

Beat the egg, blend with the potato, flour and seasonings. With floured hands shape into walnut size balls, make a hollow in each and enclose a bread cube in it. Drop the dumplings into boiling water, boil 10 minutes, drain, and add to soup.

* Saffron is stocked by chemists.

SAUCES AND GRAVIES

White Sauce

This is the basis of many varieties of sauce. First, a paste of butter and flour is prepared. This is called the *roux*. It must be stirred thoroughly and continuously. Rather less flour than fat should be used to ensure a smooth sauce.

1 oz. butter or margarine ½ pint milk
¾ oz. flour pinch each: salt and pepper

Melt the butter in a saucepan over gentle heat. Add the flour and stir vigorously for 2 minutes with a wooden spoon. Gradually stir in the milk, which may be hot or cold, then simmer and stir over gentle heat for 7 minutes to cook the flour. Off the heat, stir in the seasonings. At this stage, an extra teaspoon of butter is stirred in. Prepared in this way the sauce will be smooth and creamy.

Coating Sauce for Dishes Au Gratin

To prepare dishes *au gratin*, place the cooked food in a buttered fireproof dish, and coat the surface thinly with White Sauce. Sprinkle flaked or grated cheese over rather lavishly, scatter a few bread raspings over. Dot with butter. Place under the griller or in the oven for a few minutes to melt and slightly colour the cheese. Serve without delay.
Note 1. For a 'full' *gratin*, repeat the sauce-cheese-crumb coating of the food, before browning in the oven or under the griller. *2.* A little grated cheese may also be stirred *into* the White Sauce before coating the food if marked cheese flavour is required as in the case of Cauliflower *au Gratin*. *3.* A nice finish may be had without sauce if desired. Cover the food with flaked or grated cheese, dot with butter, brown under the griller. Bread raspings may be used for this, or omitted. *4.* The foods to be prepared *au gratin* should be moist in themselves. Stewed mushrooms, cooked broccoli, macaroni, lightly cooked tomatoes, boiled onions are all suitable. See also, Eggs Au Gratin, p. 64, and Mixed Vegetables Au Gratin, p. 48.

Sauce as an Ingredient

Cooked foods simmered in a creamy sauce are described as 'Creamed'. They do not necessarily contain cream, and the name refers to consistency rather than ingredients. A little cream stirred into the sauce or into the dish at the end of the simmering improves the dish. Vegetables, savouries and eggs are all suitable for creaming. The above remarks apply also to 'Cream Soups'. These are usually a blend of white sauce and purée in the proportion of 2 cups thin white sauce and 1 cup vegetable purée. Cream, top milk, and unsweetened evaporated milk added to soups, even in small amounts, add richness and delicacy and justify the name 'Cream Soup'.

Thick White Sauce occurs as an ingredient of certain rissoles. It binds the ingredients, blends their flavours, and imparts inner creaminess that contrasts agreeably with the crisp outer surface of the rissole.

Thick Sauce (Panada)

2 oz. butter	½ pint milk or water
2 oz. flour	pinch of salt

Melt the butter, stir in the flour, cook 2 minutes stirring, stir in the liquid, cook gently but thoroughly till the paste comes free from the sides of the pan. Use for binding rissole mixtures. A pinch of salt may be added to Panada during or after cooking.

Roux, White or Brown

2 oz. butter	2 oz. flour

For White *Roux*, melt the butter, stir in the flour and cook gently without browning. For Brown *Roux*, continue to cook the mixture gently until it is a rich brown. Dilute the *roux* with milk or vegetable stock for sauces as required.

Bechamel Sauce

This sauce consists of a savoury essence blended with White Sauce. It is said to have originated with the Marquis de Bechamel who supervised the catering at the Court of Louis XIV.

1 small onion	½ oz. butter
1 carrot	½ pint milk
2 fresh mushrooms	¾ pint white sauce
1 bouquet garni	pinch each: salt, pepper and nutmeg

Chop the vegetables very small and put them in the saucepan with the butter and seasonings. Cook gently 5 minutes without browning. Add milk and herbs and simmer 20 minutes. Strain the essence into the white sauce, simmer 5 minutes. A spoonful of cream may be stirred in at the last.

Note. To prepare Potatoes in Bechamel, slice the cooked potatoes thinly, just cover with Bechamel Sauce, cook, stirring gently, for 5 minutes. Cooked mushrooms, carrots, hard boiled eggs, broad beans and many other cooked foods may be finished in the same way.

Brown Sauce

A basic instruction in the making of White Sauce is: cook the flour and butter *without* browning them. For Brown Sauce the *roux* is cooked until lightly browned. This gives a nutty flavour to the sauce and slightly tints it. For deep brown sauce, use vegetable stock in place of milk and stir a little browning into the finished sauce. Gravy browning consists of a little heated sugar dissolved in water. When of reputable make it is quite wholesome, and since it is used very sparingly, it is economical. Yeast extract also has a slight browning effect on sauces and soups, but it is used, of course, mainly for its savoury flavour. It is an expensive product and contains, in some instances, a high proportion of common salt.

Cream Sauce

Stir 4 tablespoons of cream (or unsweetened evaporated milk) into ¾ pint Bechamel Sauce, simmer gently 3 minutes, remove from heat and stir in a teaspoon of lemon juice. (See Bechamel Sauce, p. 22.)

Mornay Sauce

Out of ½ pint White Sauce, blend a little with the beaten yolk of an egg, then gradually stir in the rest of the sauce. Reheat gently but do not boil. Before serving, stir in 2 tablespoons grated cheese.

Soubise Sauce

Cook ¾ lb. onions in ¾ pint milk till very tender. Drain when done, pass through a sieve, then stir the purée into ½ pint of hot white sauce. *Note.* If the White Sauce is fairly thick, the onion liquor may be stirred into the sauce.

Cheese Sauce

Stir 3 tablespoons grated cheese into ½ pint to ¾ pint White Sauce just before serving. Do not cook the cheese in the sauce.

D'Uxelles Sauce

The name 'D'Uxelles' is given to a mixture of chopped shallot, mushrooms, parsley and chervil lightly fried in butter and seasoned with a pinch of black pepper. It is, obviously, rich and delicious, and a spoonful or two added to a bland tasting sauce is a distinct improvement.

For the D'Uxelles Mixture

1 chopped shallot	handful each: chopped parsley
½ chopped onion	and chervil
2 mushrooms	seasoning
½ oz. butter	

Slowly fry the onion, shallot, herbs and seasoning in the butter for 5 minutes, add the minced mushrooms and cook together 5 minutes more.

For D'Uxelles Sauce

Stir the D'Uxelles mixture of the above recipe into ½ pint 'White' Sauce made with vegetable stock instead of milk. Simmer 3 minutes. Deepen colour to desired tone with a few drops of browning.

Hollandaise Sauce

yolks of 3 eggs	pinch each: salt and pepper
4 oz. butter	juice of a small lemon

Warm, but *do not melt* the butter in a basin. In another vessel, beat the yolks of the eggs with seasoning, over hot water (not boiling water). Stir in the warmed butter a little at a time, but never stop stirring. Remove from heat, gradually stir in lemon juice to taste. Serve at once in a lukewarm sauce boat. Good with asparagus, eggs, new potatoes, cauliflower, etc.

Egg and Lemon Sauce

1 egg   ¼ pint vegetable stock
1 hard-boiled egg   juice of ½ lemon

Beat the egg for 2 minutes, gradually stir in the lemon juice, whip in the stock a little at a time, stirring or whisking constantly. Cook over hot water, stirring, till the sauce thickens. Add the diced hard-boiled egg just before serving in a warm sauce boat. *Note.* If the eggs are small, use rather less than ¼ pint stock.

Mayonnaise Sauce

yolks of 2 eggs   juice of a lemon
about ¼ pint olive oil   small pinch of salt

Put the yolks and salt in a shallow basin, mix well, add the oil, drop by drop at first, stirring well all the time. Gradually stir in the oil in larger amounts, but continue to stir with vigour. When the sauce is thickened, gradually stir in lemon juice until the sauce tastes sufficiently sharp. Good with hard-boiled eggs and most salads.

Bread Sauce

½ pint milk   1 blade mace
1 herb bouquet   ½ teaspoon peppercorns
1 oz. onion   toasted bread crumbs

To prepare the crumbs, bake a slice or two of stale bread in a slow oven till very crisp, then crush fine with a rolling pin. Simmer the onion, herbs and spice in the milk for 15 minutes, but it should not boil. Strain off the flavoured hot milk into a jug, adding a little more plain hot milk if the liquor is much reduced. Stir in the crumbs gradually until the desired thickness results. A spoonful of cream is sometimes stirred in at the last. Good with various vegetables and savouries.

Curry Sauce

1 lb. onions   1 tablespoon curry powder
1 apple   1 pint thickened gravy
2 oz margarine

Slice the onions and apple and fry very slowly in the margarine till lightly coloured, then stir in the curry powder and cook gently, stirring, for 10 minutes more. Add the gravy, simmer and stir for 15 minutes. Serve hot.

Note 1. A pinch each of cinnamon, ginger and nutmeg stirred in at the last makes the sauce fragrant. *2.* Vegetables and other foods simmered in a well prepared curry sauce for ½ hour or so, become 'curries'. Fresh, uncooked vegetables are suitable for currying but they require much longer cooking. They must simmer gently (or bake in a casserole) until the vegetables are very tender, and this may take 3 hours. *3.* The sauce is equally good as an adjunct to vegetables and other dishes. (See e.g., Egg Curry, p. 65.)

Treacle Sauce

Stir 2 tablespoons black treacle into ¼ pint water, add the juice of ½ a lemon, boil 5 minutes.

Chocolate-Coffee Sauce

1 oz. cocoa
1 oz. brown sugar

½ pint black coffee
1 teaspoon butter

Put the cocoa in a basin, bring the strained, clear coffee to the boil and pour by driblets into the cocoa powder, while working it to a smooth paste. When the paste is formed, gradually stir in the rest of the coffee. Stir in the sugar, boil, then simmer 2 minutes. Remove from heat and stir in the butter. Serve hot, with sweet dishes according to taste. Good with Chocolate Pudding. (See p. 116.)

Custard Sauce

2 eggs
1 pint hot milk

½ oz. sugar
2 drops vanilla essence

Beat the eggs with the sugar in a jug, gradually stir in the hot milk, stand the jug in a pan of simmering water, stir one way with a wooden spoon till the custard is as thick as cream. Stir in the vanilla and serve hot.

Note. This is true Custard Sauce and should not be confused with Custard Powder Sauce which is prepared from custard powder, sugar, and milk, and which is quite wholesome, nutritious (because of the milk), and very popular. It is also useful in many sweet dishes for its thickening properties, and even in some savoury dishes; the vanilla flavour of the powder does not, as a rule, clash with the taste of savoury dishes in which it is used.

Apple Sauce

1 lb. apples
1 oz. butter
½ cup water
brown sugar to taste

Core, peel, and slice the apples, simmer gently with the water till pulpy, pass through the sieve, stir in the butter, sweeten to taste. Good with lentil savouries.

Horseradish Sauce

½ cup grated horseradish
¼ pint cream
1 tablespoon lemon juice
pinch each: pepper, salt and sugar

Whip the cream slightly, stir in the grated horseradish, lemon juice and seasonings. To vary, stir in a dessertspoon grated cooked beetroot.

Celery Sauce

Finely chop a well-cooked head of celery and stir into ¾ pint White Sauce. Season with a pinch of celery salt and mace.

Lemon Mint Sauce

juice of 1 lemon
1 tablespoon water
1 level teaspoon brown sugar
1 tablespoon shredded fresh mint

Mix lemon juice and water, add sugar and stir till dissolved. Wash mint well, shred fine, stir into the liquid, stand 10 minutes before use.

Zingara Sauce

1 pint haricot bean stock
¼ lb. mushrooms
2 onions
1 oz. butter
1 tablespoon flour
seasoning

Slice the mushrooms and onions and fry gently for 15 minutes in the butter. Gradually moisten with the bean stock, simmer 15 minutes, rub through sieve. Correct seasoning. Good with many savouries and vegetables. *Note.* Bean stock is prepared by soaking ½ lb. haricot beans overnight, rinsing, adding a quart of fresh water and simmering gently for 4 hours with a herb bouquet. A little yeast extract may be stirred in at the end, and the stock strained off, for use as directed.

Cashew Nut Sauce

Stir a tablespoon of Cashew Nut Butter into ½ pint white sauce just before serving, and add a pinch of minced fresh parsley.

Onion Sauce (1)

¼ lb. onions	½ pint white sauce
1 bouquet garni	seasoning

Simmer the onions with the herbs in very little water till tender, chop very fine, stir into the White Sauce with any residual cooking water. Simmer 5 minutes, season to taste. *Note.* The finished sauce may be passed through a sieve if required very smooth. A nut of butter stirred in at the last is an improvement.

Onion Sauce (2)

1 lb. onions	seasoning
1 oz. butter	

Chop the onions, put them in the casserole with the butter, add a tablespoon of hot water, cook gently 3 hours. Stir in the seasoning and a nut of fresh butter.

Tomato Sauce

½ lb. tomatoes	¼ teaspoon sugar
1 bouquet garni	pinch pepper
1 teaspoon grated onion	pinch mixed spice
1 oz. butter	1 dessertspoon cornflour
¼ teaspoon salt	½ pint vegetable stock

Quarter the tomatoes and put them in the saucepan with the other ingredients, excepting stock and cornflour. Stew gently for 20

minutes. Remove bouquet garni. Pass tomatoes, etc. through a fine sieve, and return this purée to a rinsed pan. Add stock and bring to the boil. Make a smooth paste of the cornflour with a little cold water, and pour on to it the boiling sauce, stirring well. Simmer 5 minutes before serving.

Clear Gravy

¾ pint vegetable cooking water ½ teaspoon yeast extract
1 large herb bouquet seasoning
gravy browning

Simmer the herbs in the vegetable stock for 20 minutes. Stir in the extract, seasoning and browning. Strain and serve hot. *Note 1*. A grate of raw onion juice is sometimes added at the last. *2*. Mushroom cooking liquid imparts extra savour.

Thickened Gravy

1 level dessertspoon flour ½ teaspoon grated onion
¼ oz. butter gravy browning
½ pint vegetable stock seasoning

Melt the butter, stir in the flour, cook and stir till lightly coloured. Gradually add liquid, stirring well. Simmer 5 minutes, add a few drops of browning and the grated onion.

Note 1. For Tomato Gravy stir a tablespoon of tomato purée into the gravy. *2*. For Cream Gravy, stir 2 tablespoons cream into the Thickened Gravy. *3*. Thickened Gravy may be flavoured during the simmering stage by adding either 2 mushrooms, or ½ blade mace, or a small onion stuck with 3 cloves, or 4 or 5 peppercorns, or ½ teaspoon celery salt, or a pinch of curry powder.

Onion Gravy

2 onions ½ teaspoon yeast extract
½ oz. butter seasoning
½ pint water

Chop the onions, fry slowly in the butter till *well* browned. Stir in the hot water, extract and seasoning, simmer 5 minutes, pass through sieve or strainer, reheat. *Note*. A mere speck of grated garlic simmered in the gravy gives piquancy and added flavour.

MAIN COURSE DISHES

NUT DISHES

Curried Nutmeat and Vegetable Pie

3 cups cooked mixed vegetables   ½ pint curry sauce
2 cups diced nutmeat   short crust pastry (see p. 137)

Peas, cauliflower, carrots and mushrooms make a good blend of vegetables for this dish. Celery, aubergines, tomatoes and onions is another popular choice. Turn the selected cooked vegetables into the pie dish, pour in the sauce, put on the rolled pastry top, brush with milk, bake to brown pastry and serve hot.

Vegetable Pie with Nutmeat

3 cups cooked mixed vegetables   ½ recipe Baked Nutmeat or any
1 cup fried onions   nut savoury
½ pint tomato sauce

Put the selected cooked vegetables, fried onions, and sauce in the pie dish. Spread the nutmeat mixture, unbaked, over the vegetables. Bake in a moderate oven 45 minutes. Serve hot.

Steamed Nutmeat (1)

8 oz. mixed ground nuts   ½ teaspoon salt
2 oz. gluten flour   warm water to mix
yolks of 2 eggs

Mix the nuts, gluten flour and salt. Beat the yolks of the eggs with a little water and stir in. Mix to a firm mass with as little water as possible. Turn the mixture into a greased mould, cover with greased paper, steam in the usual way for 2 hours. Stand 3 minutes before unmoulding. Serve hot with gravy or sauce, potatoes and other vegetables. This is equally nice cold with salads, or in sandwiches with a dab of mustard, or as a filling for patties with a little sauce to moisten.

Steamed Nutmeat (2)

8 oz. ground mixed nuts   1 clove garlic
8 oz. bread crumbs   1 teaspoon mixed dried herbs
2 eggs   pinch each: pepper and nutmeg
½ cup thick sauce   ½ teaspoon salt
1 cup fried onions

Finely mince the fried onions which, for this dish, are best cooked in butter. Grate the garlic. Beat the eggs. Mix all the prepared ingredients thoroughly, then turn into a well-greased mould. Cover with greased paper, then steam in the usual way, for 2 hours. Serve hot with gravy and vegetables or cold with salad.

Baked Nutmeat (1)

4 oz. ground nuts (any kind)   1 cup fried onions
4 oz. bread crumbs   ½ cup minced parsley
1 egg   ½ teaspoon celery salt
½ cup thick sauce   seasoning

Beat the egg, mix all the ingredients, turn into a well greased pie dish to a depth of 2 inches. Bake in a moderate oven 50 minutes. *Note.* Equal parts almonds and cashew nuts are good for this dish.

Baked Nutmeat (2)

6 oz. mixed ground nuts   1 cup cooked onions
2 eggs   ½ cup minced parsley
2 cups bread crumbs   pinch each: pepper and nutmeg
2 shredded wheat sections   1 level teaspoon salt

Crumble the shredded wheat with a rolling pin. Beat the eggs. Mince the cooked onions fine. Mix all the prepared ingredients, place in a greased oven dish, bake 1 hour in a moderately hot oven, Gas Mark 5, or 375 deg. Serve hot with sauce and vegetables.

Baked Hazel Nut Rissoles

4 oz. ground hazel nuts   ½ cup bread crumbs
1 egg   pinch dried thyme
1 cup boiled rice   1 teaspoon salt
1 cup fried onions

Mix all the ingredients. On a crumbed board, shape into small round cakes. Place on a well-greased baking sheet, and bake in a moderately hot oven, Gas Mark 5, or 375 deg., for ½ hour, turning, after 15 minutes, to brown both sides. Serve hot with gravy and vegetables.

Mixed Nut Rissoles

4 oz. mixed ground nuts
1 cup bread crumbs
2 shredded wheat sections
1 egg

3 cooked onions
½ cup minced parsley
¼ teaspoon salt (or to taste)
frying fat

Chop the drained cooked onions very fine. Beat the egg. Crumble the shredded wheat to powder with a rolling pin. Mix all the ingredients except fat. Shape on a crumbed board into small kite-shaped rissoles. Fry both sides in shallow hot fat, browning well. Serve hot with potatoes, peas and gravy, and an additional vegetable.

Baked Nut and Rice Croquettes

4 oz. mixed ground nuts
1 cup boiled rice
1 cup mashed potato
1 cup bread crumbs

2 eggs
1 grated raw onion
grated cheese for sprinkling
seasoning to taste

Beat the eggs, mix with all the ingredients to a firm dough, adding a little more bread crumb if necessary. Shape the mixture into small buns, sprinkle grated cheese over, place on a well-greased baking sheet, bake in a moderately hot oven, Gas Mark 5, or 375 deg., for ½ hour. Serve hot with mushroom sauce, carrots, peas and roasted potatoes.

Brazil Nut Savouries

4 oz. ground Brazil nuts
6 oz. soft bread crumbs
1 egg
1 cup thick white sauce

½ cup minced parsley
1 grated raw onion
salt, pepper and nutmeg

Beat the egg, stir into the cooled sauce, mix with the other ingredients, seasoning to taste. Grease small, individual moulds, sprinkle fine bread crumbs in, fill with the mixture, bake in a moderately hot oven, Gas Mark 5, or 375 deg., for 20 minutes. Stand 3 minutes, unmould, dish up with a border of mixed diced vegetables, and serve with baked potatoes and gravy.

Walnut Potato Cakes

4 oz. ground walnuts	½ teaspoon dried sage
2 cups dry mashed potato	1½ cups bread crumbs
½ cup fried onions	seasoning
2 eggs	frying fat
½ cup minced parsley	

Mix the ground walnuts, mashed potato, 1 beaten egg, herbs, seasoning, fried onions and 1 cup bread crumbs, form into rissoles, coat in crumbs, then in beaten egg; fry in hot fat to brown sides. Serve hot with vegetables and Thickened Gravy, or serve cold with Fruit and Vegetable Salad and wholemeal rolls and butter.

Pine Kernel and Mushroom Savoury

4 oz. milled pine kernels	4 oz. mushrooms
2 oz. ground almonds	1 tablespoon minced parsley
1 egg	pinch dried thyme
2 cups soft bread crumbs	½ teaspoon salt
1 cup thick white sauce	

Slice and simmer the mushrooms till tender. Use the cooking liquor with milk and a tablespoon of butter to make the White Sauce. Mix all the prepared ingredients. Turn mixture into a buttered baking dish. Bake in a moderately hot oven, Gas Mark 5, or 375 deg., for 40 minutes. Serve hot with tomato sauce or gravy and vegetables.

Barley Nut Roast

2 cups boiled barley	½ cup flour
1 cup ground mixed nuts	1 cup fried onions
1 cup bread crumbs	2 eggs
seasoning	½ cup thick sauce

Beat the eggs. Mix all the ingredients, pack into a well-buttered baking dish and bake in a moderately hot oven, Gas Mark 5, or

375 deg., for 45 minutes. Serve hot with potatoes, cauliflower and gravy. To vary, use peanut butter instead of nuts. Soften the peanut butter with a little hot water before mixing in.

Nutmeat Sauté

2 cups diced nutmeat (any kind)	½ lb. leeks (white part)
1 cup thick sauce	¼ lb. mushrooms
1 oz. butter	1 cup cooked peas

Stew the sliced leeks and mushrooms in the butter and a very little water till tender. Use the liquid with milk for making the sauce, add the diced nutmeat and heat very gently to warm through. Mix with peas, leeks and mushrooms and dish up in a hot dish.

Nutmeat Fritters in Rice Border

½ recipe any preferred nutmeat	grilled tomatoes
2 eggs	cooked rice for border
seasoned flour	frying fat

Cut the nutmeat into 'dominoes', coat with seasoned flour, then in beaten eggs, and fry in hot fat (or butter) turning to cook both sides brown. Pile the hot fritters in the centre of the dish with grilled tomatoes around, and bordered by hot cooked rice. Curry sauce, apple sauce, or chutney are suitable accompaniments, and fruit and vegetable salad is curiously good with the dish.

Almond and Vegetable Roast

2 cups diced cooked potatoes	1 cup bread crumbs
1 cooked carrot	2 eggs
1 cup fried onions	1 cup thick sauce
1 herb bouquet	seasoning
1 cup cooked peas	

Simmer the sauce with the herb bouquet for 10 minutes, cool, then stir in the beaten eggs and seasoning. Cut the cooked carrot and potatoes very small but do not mash, add to the bread crumbs, fried onions, peas and strained sauce. Turn the mixture into a buttered baking dish keeping it 2 inches deep. Bake in a slow to moderate oven, Gas Mark 3-4, or 335-360 deg., for 1 hour. Serve with gravy, potatoes and green salad.

Vegetable Casserole with Almond Dumplings

2 cups diced cooked potatoes
1 cup cooked peas
4 oz. mushrooms
½ lb. onions
1 cup white sauce
frying fat

For the Dumplings :
2 oz. ground almonds
2 oz. fine bread crumbs
2 oz. flour
seasoning
milk to mix

Slice and lightly brown the onions in fat, add the sliced mushrooms and cook 10 minutes more. Turn the cooked onions and mushrooms, the potatoes and peas into the casserole, pour in the sauce (enriched with vegetable cooking liquids). Mix the dumpling ingredients with just enough milk to make a firm dough, roll into walnut size balls, put them on the vegetables, cover and bake in a moderately hot oven, Gas Mark 5, or 375 deg., for about 45 minutes. Serve hot. *Note.* The vegetables used for this dish may, of course, be widely varied. Carrots, cauliflower, broccoli, broad beans, marrow, French beans, celery, asparagus and so on are very suitable. Fried onions and mushrooms, however, always provide a 'background' of savour and appetizing aroma.

Nutmeat with Baked Beans

3 cups diced nutmeat (any kind)
2 cups baked beans in tomato
1 oz. butter

2 cups stewed leeks or onions
1 oz. butter
seasoning

Turn all the ingredients into a greased casserole, add a cup of the onion or leek cooking water. Cover, and cook gently 1 hour. Serve hot.

Tomato Nut Roast

4 oz. ground mixed nuts
½ lb. tomatoes
2 cups bread crumbs
butter for dotting
1 tablespoon grated raw onion

¼ cup minced parsley and fresh
mint
2 eggs
seasoning

Peel and cut the tomatoes into small dice. Beat the eggs. Mix all the ingredients and pack the mixture in a buttered pie dish. Dot with butter. Bake in a moderately hot oven, Gas Mark 5, or 375 deg., for ½ hour. Serve hot with vegetables. Nice cold for sandwiches or with salads.

Nut and Vegetable Loaf

6 oz. ground mixed nuts
6 oz. bread crumbs
2 eggs
2 cups stewed celery, mushroom
 and onion

½ cup minced parsley
½ teaspoon salt
pepper and nutmeg to taste

Drain the cooked vegetables and chop fine. Beat the eggs. Mix all the prepared ingredients, shape into a roll, wrap twice in greased paper and screw the ends tight, then tie with tape. Bake on a greased dish in a moderately hot oven, Gas Mark 5, or 375 deg., for 1 hour. Serve hot with gravy and vegetables, or sliced, cold, with salad.

Cashew and Almond Roast

2 oz. ground cashew nuts
2 oz. ground almonds
1 cup cooked rice
1 cup soft bread crumbs
1 egg

2 onions
½ cup chopped parsley
frying fat
salt, pepper and pinch dried
 thyme

Chop the onions and fry slowly till pale brown, remove from heat and mix with all the remaining ingredients. Pack the mixture 2 inches deep in a well-greased pie dish. Bake 40 minutes in a moderately hot oven, Gas Mark 5, or 375 deg. Serve hot with gravy and vegetables, or cold with salad.

Cashew Nut and Celery Croquettes

4 oz. ground cashew nuts
1 heart celery
4 oz. bread crumbs
1 dessertspoon grated onion

1 egg
½ teaspoon dried mixed herbs
½ teaspoon salt
grated cheese to sprinkle

Slice the celery and stew till tender. Beat the egg. Mix all the ingredients, shape into small buns and place these on a well-greased baking-sheet, sprinkled with grated cheese. Bake in a hot oven, Gas Mark 6, or 400 deg., for 25 minutes. Serve hot with gravy and vegetables.

Peanut Roast

4 oz. ground peanuts
2 eggs
2 cups bread crumbs
½ lb. onions
½ teaspoon mixed dried herbs

½ teaspoon salt
pinch each: nutmeg and pepper
fat for frying and dotting
¼ pint vegetable stock

Chop and fry the onions. Beat the eggs. Mix all the prepared ingredients and turn the mixture into a well-greased baking dish to a depth of 1½ inches. Bake 45 minutes in a moderately hot oven, Gas Mark 5, or 375 deg. Serve hot with Thickened Gravy and potatoes, and either cabbage, sprouts, spinach or cauliflower. Also good cold with wholemeal bread and butter and salad.

PEAS, BEANS, LENTILS

Lentil Roast

8 oz. red lentils
4 to 6 oz. cheese
1 egg
2 oz. bread crumbs
6 oz. onions
frying fat

½ cup minced parsley
¼ teaspoon dried thyme
1 clove garlic
1 teaspoon salt
dash of pepper and nutmeg
½ cup vegetable stock

Simmer washed lentils in ½ pint water 25 minutes, when water will have been absorbed. Chop onions fine, grate garlic, slowly fry both together till well browned. Flake the cheese. Beat egg. Mix all the prepared ingredients and turn the mixture into a well-greased oven dish. Bake in a moderately hot oven, Gas Mark 5, or 375 deg., for 35 to 40 minutes. Serve hot with gravy and vegetables.

Stuffed Lentil Roast

1 recipe Lentil Roast mixture

For the stuffing :

1 cup cooked vermicelli
2 oz. grated cheese

½ cup bread crumbs
pinch dried herbs
seasoning

Mix the ingredients for the stuffing. Put half the Lentil Roast mixture in a greased baking dish, spread the stuffing over, cover with the rest of the lentil mixture. Bake as directed for Lentil Roast (above). Serve hot with potatoes, greens and sauce or thick gravy.

Lentil and Potato Rissoles

½ lb. red lentils	1 cup bread crumbs
2 oz. grated cheese	1 cup fried onions
1 egg	1 bouquet garni
1 teaspoon yeast extract	seasoning
½ pint dry mashed potato	frying fat and raspings

Cook lentils as for Lentil Roast (above), beat egg, dissolve yeast extract in a spoonful of hot water. Mix the prepared ingredients, form the mixture into rissoles, roll in fine bread raspings, fry brown on both sides in shallow hot fat. Serve hot with gravy and vegetables.

Lentil and Tomato Paté

8 oz. red lentils	1 cup fried onions
6 oz. flaked cheese	1 clove grated garlic
2 beaten eggs	½ cup minced parsley
2 pulped tomatoes	1 teaspoon salt
1 bay leaf	pinch each: pepper, nutmeg and
1 cup bread crumbs	curry powder

Add bay leaf to lentils and cook as in recipe for Lentil Roast (above). Mix the cooked lentils with the beaten eggs, add all the remaining ingredients and stir well. Turn the mixture into a well-greased baking dish and bake in a moderately hot oven, Gas Mark 5, or 375 deg., for 45 minutes. Serve hot with sauce or thick brown gravy, potatoes and greens, or serve cold with salads or in sandwiches. The cold paté may also be used as a filling for pastry patty cases. For a teatime spread, blend a cup of the paté with a grated hard-boiled egg and a dab of made mustard.

Rice and Lentil Savoury

4 oz. rice	1 tablespoon minced parsley
2 oz. red lentils	1 clove minced garlic
1 egg	1 teaspoon salt
1 cup fried onions	dash of pepper and nutmeg
2 oz. flaked cheese	½ oz. fat

Cook the rice till tender, then drain, stir in the fat and half the beaten egg. Cook lentils and drain, then mix with rest of the beaten egg, fried onions, cheese, parsley and seasonings. Put half the rice mixture in a well-greased pie dish, add the lentil mixture, spread the remaining rice over the top. Bake in a moderately hot oven, Gas Mark 5, or 375 deg., for ½ hour. Serve hot with cooked greens.

Savoury Sausages

1 cup cooked red lentils
2 cups cooked rice (raw rice swells to 3 times its volume when cooked)
1 tablespoon tomato extract
2 hard-boiled eggs

1 beaten egg
bread raspings
frying fat
seasoning and ½ teaspoon dried herbs

Grate the hard-boiled eggs, mix with the *cold* cooked rice, cooked lentils, seasonings and extract. Shape into sausages, coat in egg and bread raspings, fry, browning evenly, in hot fat. Serve hot with mashed or fried potatoes. *Note.* The seasoning consists of a salt-spoon each of ginger, cinnamon, curry powder and salt.

Lentil Stuffed Tomatoes

6 even sized tomatoes
1 hard-boiled egg

½ recipe Lentil Roast
grated cheese to sprinkle

Slice stem end of the tomatoes, and remove sufficient pulp to leave firm cases. Mix the removed pulp with the grated hard-boiled egg and the mashed Lentil Roast. Fill the tomato cases with the mixture, and roll surplus stuffing into walnut size balls with bread crumbs to make them firm. Put the stuffed tomatoes and savoury balls on a well-greased baking tin and bake in a hot oven, Gas Mark 6, or 400 deg., for 20 minutes. Serve hot with potatoes and peas. Also nice cold with salad and brown bread and butter.

Lentil Fritters

1 cup cooked red lentils
2 cups cooked rice
½ cup thick curry sauce
1 egg
2 oz. flaked cheese

1 teaspoon salt
pinch each: pepper and nutmeg
coating batter
frying fat

Mix all the ingredients except coating batter and frying fat, and stand the mixture in a cold place until quite firm. Cut into neat wedges, lift each with a fork and coat with batter, fry golden brown in hot fat. Serve hot with cooked carrots, cabbage or peas, potatoes, etc. (See Frying Batter, p. 155.)

Lentil Mince with Mashed Potatoes

1 cup cooked red lentils (4 oz. raw)
1 cup cooked rice
1 cup fried onions
4 oz. tomatoes
4 oz. mushrooms
1 beaten egg
1 hard-boiled egg
2 oz. flaked cheese
1 small teaspoon salt
mashed potatoes

Stew the sliced mushrooms and diced tomatoes till tender, stir in the fried onions, cooked lentils, cooked rice, diced hard-boiled egg and seasoning. Stir over boiling water till thoroughly hot, remove from heat and stir in the flaked cheese. Dish up on a hot platter, within a border of hot mashed potatoes which have been blended with the beaten egg and placed in a hot oven for a few minutes.

Zingara Casserole

1½ pints cooked butter beans *or*
1 lb canned beans
¼ lb. mushrooms
¾ lb. button onions
¾ pint white sauce
1 clove garlic
1 teaspoon yeast extract
1 herb bouquet
1 small teaspoon salt
pinch each: pepper and nutmeg
1½ oz. butter

Put prepared onions, sliced mushrooms, herbs, seasoning and butter in the stewpan and cook gently till very tender, then stir in extract and seasoning. Add the cooked beans and the sauce, cover and cook gently ½ hour. Serve hot with grated cheese and mashed potatoes. *Note.* Edible fungi such as chanterelles, boletus and puff balls may replace the mushrooms in this dish.

Egg and Pea Kromeskis

batter for 8 small pancakes
2 hard-boiled eggs
1 cup cooked peas
1 tablespoon grated cheese
1 cup Bechamel sauce
½ teaspoon salt
pinch each: pepper and nutmeg
frying fat

Cook the pancakes on one side only and keep ready. Chop the eggs coarsely, mix with the cooked peas, a little of the sauce and seasoning. Put a spoonful of the mixture in the centre of the cooked side of each pancake, then fold each into a three-cornered package with the edges overlapping at the centre. Fry in hot fat, turn to brown both sides, drain and serve hot with the sauce. *Note.* The Kromeskis may be baked instead of fried, but in this case, pour the sauce (or gravy) into the dish containing the Kromeskis before baking ½ hour in a moderately hot oven, Gas Mark 5, or 375 deg. (See Pancakes, p. 156.)

Butter Bean Savouries with Spinach

2 cups sieved, cooked butter beans (8 oz. when uncooked)	½ cup cheese sauce
	½ teaspoon salt
1 oz. ground almonds	dash each: pepper and nutmeg
1 egg	spinach
1½ cups bread crumbs	

Beat the egg with the seasonings. Mix with all the prepared ingredients and form into round cakes. Bake on a well-greased tin in a moderately hot oven, Gas Mark 5, or 375 deg., turning to brown both sides. Dish on a hot platter with a mound of hot sieved spinach in the centre, and garnished with lightly baked tomato halves.

Butter Bean Rissoles

½ lb. butter beans	1 cup fried onion
1 egg	½ teaspoon dried mixed herbs
1 oz. cheese	pepper, nutmeg and salt
½ cup boiled rice	

Scald beans, remove skins, put in a saucepan, cover with boiling water, simmer 1 hour or till quite tender, then mash smooth. Mix mashed beans with the rest of the ingredients, shape into small round cakes, place in a well-greased oven dish and bake in a moderately hot oven, Gas Mark 5, or 375 deg., for 40 minutes, turning to brown both sides. Serve hot with grilled tomatoes and cauliflower. *Note 1.* Canned beans may be used in place of the dry butter beans. *2.* Butter beans may be cooked in a pressure cooker for this dish. *3.* The rissoles may be fried in shallow, hot fat, if an oven is not available.

Butter Bean, Egg and Onion Curry

2 cups cooked butter beans	½ lb. tomatoes
1 lb. onions	1 level dessertspoon curry powder
4 oz. margarine	
1 apple	1 pint vegetable stock

Slice and fry the onions in the margarine till pale gold, stir in the curry powder and cook 5 minutes more, stir in the diced apple and tomatoes and cook together for a further 10 minutes, then turn all into a casserole. Pour in the stock. Add the cooked beans. Cook gently for 1 hour. Serve hot with rice, chutney and grated cheese. *Note.* To vary: add a spoonful of seedless raisins and a cup of diced cooked carrot when the stock is added.

Haricot and Vegetable Hot Pot

2 cups baked beans (or 1 large tin)
1 egg
½ lb. carrots
½ lb. leeks (white part)

1 cup thick sauce
1 teaspoon yeast extract
½ oz. grated cheese
seasoning

Simmer the sliced carrots and leeks till tender, and use the cooking water to make the sauce. Cool the sauce, and gradually stir in the beaten egg. Put a layer of the cooked beans in a greased hot pot dish, add the cooked carrots and leeks, cover with the rest of the beans, pour in the sauce, sprinkle the grated cheese in. Bake in a moderately hot oven, Gas Mark 5, or 375 deg., for 1 hour.

Butter Bean and Tomato Casserole

1 pint cooked butter beans
½ lb. tomatoes
¼ lb. macaroni

2 oz. grated cheese
2 oz. butter

Soak and cook the beans in soft water till tender, or cook in pressure cooker, or use tinned beans. Boil the macaroni very tender, drain, toss in the butter 5 minutes. Mix cooked beans and cooked macaroni, with diced peeled tomatoes and turn into a greased casserole. Cook gently 35 minutes. Sprinkle grated cheese on when serving.

Curried Bean, Mushroom and Tomato Pie

2 cups cooked haricot or butter beans
½ lb. sliced peeled tomatoes
1 onion
butter for frying

¼ lb. mushrooms
1 cup curry sauce
short crust pastry
seasoning

Slice and fry onion in butter, and when lightly tinted, add the sliced mushrooms and cook together 5 minutes more. Mix in the cooked beans, sliced tomatoes and seasoning, and turn into a greased pie dish. Pour in the curry sauce. Moisten edge and affix the rolled pastry top. Bake in a hot oven to brown pastry. Note: See Curry Sauce, p. 25.

Egg and Bean Turnovers

1 tin tomato beans
2 hard-boiled eggs

short crust pastry
pepper, salt and nutmeg to taste

Roll out the pastry, cut into rounds 4 inches in diameter, put a portion of the blended diced eggs, beans and seasonings in the centre of each round. Brush edges with milk and fold over into turnovers. Indent with a cup, ½ inch from edge of turnover. Brush with water, milk or beaten egg. Bake in a pastry oven to brown pastry. Good hot or cold.

Brown Bean, Egg and Mushroom Sauté

2 cups cooked brown beans
2 hard-boiled eggs
1 onion

½ lb. mushrooms
1 pint Bechamel sauce
herb bouquet

Thickly slice the larger mushrooms. Leave small ones whole. Stew gently with a little water, the herbs and the chopped onion, till tender. Dice the hard-boiled eggs. Mix hot, cooked beans, mushrooms and eggs, turn into a hot buttered dish and pour the sauce over. Serve hot. Fried potatoes and green salad are good accompaniments. *Note.* The beans should be carefully purchased to ensure that they are reasonably fresh.

Haricot Roast

1 pint cooked haricot beans
2 eggs
1 cup fried chopped onions
1 cup soft bread crumbs

2 tablespoons grated cheese
½ teaspoon salt
pinch each: pepper and nutmeg

Sieve the cooked beans, beat the eggs, mix all the prepared ingredients. Pack the mixture, 2 inches deep, in a greased pie dish. Bake in a moderately hot oven, Gas Mark 5, or 375 deg., for 40 minutes. Serve hot with grilled or baked tomatoes, cauliflower and potatoes. When cold the roast makes nice sandwiches and is tasty with salad and bread and butter.

CHEESE DISHES

Cheese Casserole

8 thin slices wholemeal bread	2 eggs
6 oz. grated Cheddar cheese	½ pint milk
2 oz. cream or curd cheese	pinch each: pepper and salt
1 dessertspoon cornflour	½ oz. butter

Blend the grated cheese with the cream cheese or curd cheese. Make a smooth paste of the cornflour with a little cold milk and mix with the blended cheeses. Spread the mixture thickly on the sliced bread and place in the casserole. Beat the eggs with the milk and a little seasoning, and pour in. Dot with the butter. Stand 10 minutes, then bake in a moderately hot oven, Gas Mark 5, or 375 deg., for ½ hour. Serve hot. Stewed leeks, baked tomatoes or braised celery are good with it.

Egg and Cheese Rissoles

1 cup mashed potato	3 oz. grated cheese
1 cup cooked rice	1 hard-boiled egg
1 cup bread crumbs	½ cup fried onions
seasoning	frying fat

Grate the hard-boiled egg. Mix all the ingredients except fat. Shape rissoles on a crumbed board. Fry in deep, hot fat to brown both sides. Serve hot with tomato sauce or casseroled onions.

Rice Cheese Savoury

4 oz. grated cheese	3 stewed tomatoes
1 oz. roasted cashew nuts	3 cups boiled rice
2 eggs	seasoning
1 cup fried onions	

Beat the eggs. Cut the tomatoes fine. Chop the nuts coarsely. Mix all the ingredients, spread the mixture ½ inch deep in a buttered baking tin. Bake in a moderately hot oven, Gas Mark 5, or 375 deg., for 20 minutes. Cut into squares, pile on a hot dish, pour tomato sauce over. Serve hot.

Cheese Rissoles (1)

4 oz. wholemeal bread
4 oz. grated cheese
2 oz. flour
2 eggs
½ pint milk

pinch of dried thyme
pinch each: pepper, salt and
   nutmeg
bread crumbs for coating
frying fat

Dice the bread, heat milk and pour over, stand 10 minutes, mash smooth. Stir in the flour, cheese, herbs and seasonings. Beat one of the eggs and stir in. Cook 5 minutes over gentle heat, stirring constantly. Spread the mixture 1 inch deep on a plate and stand 1 hour. Cut into wedges, coat in crumbs, then in beaten egg, and again in bread crumbs. Fry in hot fat to brown sides. Serve hot.

Cheese Rissoles (2)

2 cups boiled rice
1 cup fried onions
2 tomatoes
2 oz. grated cheese
1 egg

1 cup bread crumbs
pinch each: dried thyme and
   seasoning
frying fat

Peel the tomatoes and chop fine. Beat the egg. Mix all the prepared ingredients except fat. Stand the mixture until firm, then shape into rissoles on a crumbed board. Fry in hot fat, browning both sides.

Cheese Tart

6 oz. grated cheese
3 oz. butter
2 oz. flour
1 egg

½ pint milk
pinch each: salt and pepper
short crust pastry dough

Roll out the pastry and line a greased tart plate or dish. Cream the butter, stir in flour, then cream up again. Gradually pour boiling milk into the flour mixture, stirring constantly. Stir in the cheese and the seasoning. Gradually stir in the beaten egg. Cook gently, while stirring, for 3 minutes. Pour into the pastry shell. Bake in a moderate oven till pastry is done. Serve hot. Stewed celery is good with this.

Parmesan Soufflé

4 oz. grated Parmesan cheese	¼ pint milk
4 eggs	2¾ oz. flour
white of 1 egg	3 oz. butter
fine bread crumbs	pinch each: pepper and nutmeg

Melt the butter in a saucepan, stir in the flour, cook and stir over gentle heat for 2 minutes. Add the milk gradually and stir constantly over gentle heat till smooth and thickened. *Remove* from the heat, cool slightly, then add the yolks of the eggs singly, beating each well in. Stir in the cheese and the seasonings. Whip the whites of the eggs to a stiff froth and fold in. Pour into a soufflé case lined with a buttered paper extending 3 inches above the edge of the dish. Sprinkle a few bread crumbs over. Bake in a hot oven, 420 deg., for about 25 minutes. Serve immediately. Delicate vegetables such as peas, celery, asparagus tips, and tomatoes are good accompaniments. *Note.* The soufflé may be baked in a deep, greased pie dish if room enough is allowed for it to rise. See p. 104.

Cheese, Egg and Potato Pie

2 lb. cooked potatoes	1 pint white sauce
3 hard-boiled eggs	1 teaspoon celery salt
6 oz. grated cheese	pinch each: pepper and mace

Dice the hard-boiled eggs and mix with the thickly sliced potatoes. Put in the buttered pie dish. Sprinkle seasoning over. Stir 4 oz. of the cheese into the sauce and pour into the dish. Sprinkle the rest of the cheese over the sauce. For a rich dish, dot with butter, and for a brown top, sprinkle a few bread crumbs over. Bake in a hot oven, Gas Mark 7, or 425 deg., for ½ hour.

Cheese Potatoes with Poached Eggs

2 lb. boiled 'jacket' potatoes	2 oz. butter
½ lb. flaked cheese	minced parsley
1 cup cream or evaporated milk	poached eggs

Peel the potatoes, slice thickly, put a layer in a buttered casserole. Cover the potatoes thickly with flaked cheese, dot with butter, sprinkle parsley over, adding if liked a pinch of nutmeg or mace. Repeat the layers until the casserole is full, reserving cheese and butter for the top layer. Before adding the top layer, pour in the cream or evaporated milk. Bake in a moderate oven 25 minutes. Serve with poached eggs.

Cheese Savoury in Sauce

6 oz. stale wholemeal bread
6 oz. grated cheese
2 eggs
1 tablespoon grated onion
½ pint milk

¼ pint evaporated milk
3 oz. flour
pinch each: salt, pepper and mace
Bechamel sauce to serve

Dice the bread, put in a saucepan, pour in the hot milk, mash very smooth. Stir in the beaten eggs, flour, evaporated milk, cheese, onion and seasonings. Bake 45 minutes in a slow to moderate oven. Cut into squares, pile in a hot platter, pour Bechamel Sauce around. Serve with mixed vegetables.

Bread and Cheese Savoury

6 oz. grated cheese
3 eggs
¾ pint milk
6 oz. bread crumbs

2 oz. butter (melted)
pinch each: pepper, salt and mace

Beat the yolks of the eggs, stir in the rest of the ingredients excepting the whites of the eggs, and mix well. Beat the whites of the eggs to a stiff froth and fold in. Half fill a buttered casserole with the mixture (to allow for rising) and bake in a moderate oven for ½ hour. Serve at once with mashed potatoes and peas, or any other choice of vegetables.

Savoury Curd Cheese Flan

½ lb. curd cheese
2 eggs
3 tablespoons cream
1 teaspoon cornflour

¼ teaspoon salt
pinch of pepper
short crust pastry

Roll out the pastry and line a greased Victoria sandwich tin. Add cornflour, seasonings and cream to the cheese, and blend very smooth, gradually stir in the beaten eggs. Pour into the pastry flan. Bake in a moderate oven, Gas Mark 4, or 350 deg., for 35 to 40 minutes. Serve hot with grilled tomatoes and peas, or cold with salad.

Cheese Pie

sliced bread and butter for lining dish
6 oz. cheese
2 eggs

1 small onion
2 tablespoons bread crumbs
1 pint milk
pinch each: salt and pepper

Line a buttered pie dish with the bread and butter. Beat the eggs with the seasonings, stir in the grated onion, 5 oz. of flaked cheese and the milk. Pour into the lined dish and stand ½ hour. Grate the rest of the cheese, mix with the bread crumbs and sprinkle on. Bake in a slow oven, Gas Mark 3, or 335 deg., for 40 minutes. Serve hot with onion sauce and vegetables.

Mixed Vegetables Au Gratin

1 cooked cauliflower (large)	6 oz. flaked cheese
1 lb. sliced cooked potatoes	1 oz. butter
1 cup diced cooked carrots	½ cup bread raspings
2 cups cooked peas	seasoning
1 pint white sauce	

Make a border of the potatoes in a *large*, greased baking dish, put the neatly divided cauliflower in the centre, and fill the remaining space with the mixed carrots and peas. Stir 1 oz. of the flaked cheese into the sauce and pour over the vegetables. Sprinkle the rest of the flaked cheese over the vegetables, sprinkle the bread raspings over, dot with the butter, bake in a hot oven 8 minutes. Serve hot. Dry toast is good with it.

Italian Cheese Savoury

4 oz. semolina	1 egg
½ oz. butter (and extra for dotting)	4 oz. grated cheese
	pinch each: salt and nutmeg
1 pint milk	

Put the milk, butter, salt and nutmeg in a saucepan, bring to the boil, sprinkle in the semolina, cook and stir over gentle heat till the mixture is thick and comes free from the pan sides. Remove from heat, stir in 1 oz. of the cheese, then the beaten egg. Spread the mixture on a board wetted with water, to set firm, then cut into small squares, stack them on a buttered dish, sprinkled with the rest of the cheese. Dot with the extra butter, bake in a quick oven for 5 minutes, or toast under the griller.

Cheese Pudding (1)

6 oz. grated cheese	½ pint evaporated milk (unsweetened)
2 eggs	
2 tablespoons melted butter	½ pint milk
1 pint bread crumbs	pinch of salt and ground mace

Blend the milks, pour into the beaten eggs gradually, stirring well. Stir in the bread crumbs, cheese, melted butter and seasonings. Stand the dish in a tin of hot water, bake in a slow oven, Gas Mark 3, or 335 deg., for about 1 hour. Serve hot with nicely cooked green vegetables.

Cheese Pudding (2)

4 oz. flaked cheese	1 pint milk
2 eggs	½ teaspoon celery salt
4 oz. bread crumbs	pinch each: pepper, nutmeg and
1 oz. butter	mustard

Heat the milk and pour over the bread crumbs. Stir in the butter, seasonings, cheese, and well-beaten eggs. Pour into a greased dish and bake in a moderately hot oven, Gas Mark 5, or 375 deg., for ½ hour. Serve with creamed vegetables.

Cheese Pudding (Steamed)

3 oz. flour	4 oz. grated cheese
¼ pint milk	2 eggs
pinch of salt	2 oz. butter

Put milk, butter and salt in a saucepan, bring to the boil, stir in the flour, cook and stir over gentle heat till the paste comes free from the pan. Remove from heat, cool, beat in the eggs one at a time. Beat in the grated cheese. Turn the mixture into a buttered pudding basin, cover with greased paper, steam 1 hour. Serve with gravy and vegetables.

Cheese Bondons

⅜ pint water	2 eggs
2 oz. butter	2 oz. grated cheese
pinch of salt	2 oz. cream cheese
5 oz. flour	2 tablespoons cream
1 cup bread crumbs	parsley

Put the water, butter and salt in a saucepan, boil, stir in flour, cook and stir till the paste comes free from the pan. Remove from heat, cool, stir in the eggs singly, stir in the bread crumbs and cheese. Stand ½ hour, roll into egg size balls, place on a greased baking tin, then bake the Bondons in a moderately hot oven for 25 minutes. Cut a slit in the top of each, and put in a spoonful of the cream cheese blended with the cream. Dish on a hot plate, garnish with parsley, serve hot, with tomato gravy, i.e. ½ pint clear gravy simmered 3 minutes with 2 tablespoons sieved tomato.

Cheese Fritters

3 oz. grated cheese	2 oz. flour
4 oz. wholemeal bread crumbs	½ pint milk
1 egg and 1 yolk of egg	1 oz. butter
frying batter	frying fat

Simmer the milk and bread crumbs for 3 minutes, gradually stir in the flour, remove from the heat, stir in the grated cheese, stir in the egg and the yolk, stir in the butter. Coat tablespoons of the mixture in batter and fry brown in hot fat. (For Frying Batter see 'Miscellaneous Recipes,' p. 155.)

VEGETABLE MAIN DISHES

Vegetable Platter with Eggs

cooked peas	fried onion rings
grilled tomatoes	poached or fried eggs
grilled mushrooms	

Dish up the assortment neatly, serve very hot, with potato chips or sauté potatoes, and tomato sauce. The onion rings may be very thick and slowly fried till pale gold, or thinly sliced, sprinkled with flour, and fried quickly in deep hot fat. The former will be luscious and soft, the latter crisp.

Rice, Cheese and Tomato Pie

3 cups cooked rice	1 cup bread crumbs
1 cup tomato purée	1 cup grated cheese
1 oz. butter	seasoning
2 eggs	

Beat the eggs with a pinch of seasoning, stir into the cooked rice, put half in a buttered pie dish. Sprinkle with cheese, bread crumbs and seasoning, dab with tomato purée, dot with butter. Repeat once, then bake in a moderate oven 50 minutes. Serve hot with Cheese Sauce or Tomato Sauce.

Cauliflower and Egg Savoury

1 large cauliflower, cooked	1 beaten egg
¼ lb. each: tomatoes, mush-rooms and shallots	1 cup white sauce
	grated cheese and bread crumbs
1 oz. butter	herbs and seasoning
2 hard-boiled eggs	

Stew the sliced tomatoes, mushrooms and shallots with the butter and a bunch of herbs till soft. Cool slightly then remove herbs and stir in the beaten egg, seasoning, and a grate of nutmeg. Spread in a buttered dish. Cover with sprigs of cooked cauliflower, then add a layer of the sliced hard-boiled eggs. Pour the sauce over, sprinkle with bread crumbs, then with grated cheese. Dot with butter. Brown lightly in a quick oven or under the griller. Serve with roast potatoes and Cheese Sauce.

Nutmeat, Onion and Potato Pie

½ lb. diced nutmeat	½ pint thick brown gravy
1 lb. cooked potatoes	short crust pastry
2 cooked onions	

Slice the cooked onions and potatoes, put both in the pie dish with the nutmeat and well-seasoned gravy. Cover with the thinly rolled pastry, brush with milk, bake in a moderate oven till the pastry browns. Serve hot. *Note.* The cooking water of the onions and potatoes is, of course, best for the gravy. (See p. 31 for nutmeat recipes.)

Stuffed Potato Cakes

1 pint dry mashed potato	1 egg
1 tablespoon grated onion	bread crumbs for coating
1 tablespoon flour	fat for frying
1 cup nutmeat mixture	

Stir flour and grated onion into the mashed potato, and place dessertspoons of the mixture on a well-crumbed board. Put a marble of the nutmeat mixture on each, cover with another dessertspoon of potato, coat in beaten egg then in bread crumbs, fry in deep hot fat. Serve hot with peas and Lemon Mint Sauce. (See p. 27.)

Marrow and Mushroom Savoury

1 small vegetable marrow
4 oz. mushrooms
1 heart celery
1 onion

4 oz. cheese
1 egg
butter for dotting and stewing

Slice the mushrooms, celery and onion, stew with a little water and a pat of butter till tender. Boil the marrow, whole, for 20 minutes, cool, peel, cut into rings. Beat the egg and mix with the drained celery, mushrooms and onion. Put half the marrow rings in a buttered pie dish, spread the vegetable batter over, cover with thinly sliced cheese and the rest of the marrow. Sprinkle 1 oz. of grated cheese over, dot with butter. Bake ½ hour in a moderate oven. Serve hot with mashed potatoes.

Vegetable Curry with Lentil Noisettes

2 lb. mixed fresh vegetables
1 lb. potatoes
Lentil Roast mixture (½ recipe)

1 pint curry sauce
cooked rice

Prepare the raw, fresh, vegetables (the more kinds the better), put them in a saucepan, cover with cold water, bring slowly to the boil, simmer 20 minutes then drain; use the cooking liquid for the curry sauce. Put the simmered vegetables in a buttered casserole, and pour in the sauce. Form the Lentil Roast mixture into walnut size balls and place on the vegetables. Cook gently 3 hours. Serve hot with rice and chutney or Apple Sauce. Note: See Curry Sauce, p. 25.

Vegetables and Eggs Au Gratin

1 lb. casseroled small onions
1 cup cooked peas
1 cup mashed potatoes
4 hard-boiled eggs

½ pint Bechamel sauce
bread crumbs and grated cheese
    to sprinkle

Line a buttered pie dish with the mashed potatoes, turn in the casseroled onions and peas, put the sliced hard-boiled eggs on, pour in the sauce. Sprinkle with fine bread crumbs then with grated cheese. Brown lightly under the griller. Serve hot.

Potato Cheese Savoury

2 lb. sliced cooked potatoes $\frac{1}{4}$ pint milk
1 cup fried onions   butter for dotting
$\frac{1}{4}$ lb. flaked cheese   seasoning
2 eggs

Put layers of the sliced cooked potatoes in a well-greased casserole, spreading each layer with flaked cheese, fried onions, and a dusting of seasoning. Beat the eggs with the milk and pour in. Dot with butter. Bake in a moderate oven $1\frac{1}{4}$ hours.

Egg and Vegetable Savoury

4 cooked onions   2 eggs
4 cooked potatoes   1 oz. butter
2 cooked carrots   1 cup cheese sauce
$\frac{1}{4}$ lb. tomatoes   seasoning
1 cup cooked peas

Slice the cooked potatoes and carrots, dice the tomatoes, and add all to the cooked onions. Stir in the peas and the butter. Beat the eggs with seasoning, stir into the cheese sauce and add. Turn into a greased casserole, bake $\frac{1}{2}$ hour in a moderate oven. Serve hot.

Vegetable Casserole with Nut Dumplings

For the Casserole: *For the Nut Dumplings:*
1 lb. small potatoes   2 oz. ground nuts
$\frac{1}{2}$ lb. small onions   2 oz bread crumbs
$\frac{1}{2}$ lb. leeks   1 oz flour
1 cup diced carrots   beaten egg
seasoning $\frac{1}{2}$ pint sauce

Neatly prepare and cook the vegetables in the first column with water to cover and seasoning for 20 minutes. Drain, and turn vegetables into a casserole. Cover with White Sauce made of the vegetable cooking water. Mix the dumpling ingredient using just enough beaten egg to bind the ingredients. Roll into small balls, place on the vegetables. Cover and cook gently 1 hour.

Vegetable and Nutmeat Curry

4 cups cooked vegetables   2 cups diced nutmeat
1 pint rich curry sauce   cooked rice

Mix cooked vegetables and diced nutmeat and turn into a well-greased casserole. Pour in the sauce. Cook gently 2 hours. Serve hot with cooked rice and a salad of sliced tomatoes, sliced bananas and seedless raisins sprinkled with chopped parsley. Either cooked or uncooked nutmeat may be used for this dish. If uncooked, roll into small balls before adding to the casserole. *Note.* Instead of cooked vegetables, raw fresh vegetables may be used. Cook raw vegetable curry 3 hours.

Nutmeat Risotto

6 oz. rice	3 onions
2 cups diced nutmeat	2 oz. mushrooms
2 tomatoes	1 herb bouquet
2 oz. butter	seasoning

Slice the onions, brown lightly in the butter, add the washed and dried rice and cook and stir 5 minutes. Add the sliced mushrooms, diced tomatoes, herbs and seasoning, and turn into a casserole or stewpan. Pour in 1 cup vegetable cooking water. Cover and cook gently ½ hour or till the water is absorbed. Remove herbs, add the diced nutmeat, heat through. Serve hot, sprinkled with grated cheese.

Vegetable Cutlets

1 cup each: cooked peas, cooked carrots, cooked red lentils, mashed potato and fried onions	2 cups bread crumbs
	1 egg
	1 teaspoon salt
	1 teaspoon yeast extract

Chop the cooked ingredients very fine. Beat the egg with salt and mix in. Dissolve the extract in a spoonful of hot water and stir in. Form into cutlet shapes. Bake on a well-greased tin in a hot oven, Gas Mark 6, or 400 deg., to brown both sides, or fry in hot fat. Serve hot with gravy and greens.

Chestnut and Mushroom Ragoût

1 lb. chestnuts	4 stalks celery
¼ lb. mushrooms	1 teaspoon yeast extract
½ lb. potatoes	1 bay leaf
1 cup Bechamel sauce	seasoning

Slit the skins of the chestnuts, roast 15 minutes in a hot oven, peel and remove husks. Cut up the vegetables and put in the casserole with the chestnuts, bay leaf and seasonings, add a cup of water with the extract dissolved in it. Simmer 2 hours. Add the sauce and cook 15 minutes more.

Vegetable Dinner (1)

stuffed mushrooms   peas
chipped potatoes   tomatoes

Fill the mushroom caps with Lentil Roast mixture and bake on a greased tin for 25 minutes. Lightly bake halved tomatoes at the same time. Add a pat of fresh butter to the peas and sprinkle shredded fresh mint over. Dish on a hot platter. Serve hot.

Vegetable Dinner (2)

casseroled button onions   creamed potatoes
pea and walnut tartlets   cauliflower au gratin
carrot fritters

Cook the onions with a spoonful or two of water, a bay leaf, and a pat of butter. Cook them very slowly. When quite tender, stir in a teaspoon of yeast extract dissolved in a little hot water. Simmer thickly sliced cooked potatoes in unsweetened, evaporated milk, or in creamy white sauce, for 5 minutes. Coat long slices of cooked carrot in seasoned flour then in batter, brown in butter and keep hot. Cover baked short crust base with a mixture of cooked peas, chopped walnuts, shredded mint and beaten egg to bind, put in the oven till the egg sets, then cut into small squares. Arrange the various items on a hot dish and garnish with olives and cress.

Vegetable Dinner (3)

For the Fritters:

carrot and swede medley   ½ lb. small tomatoes
3 cups sauté potatoes   ½ lb. onions
                             2 eggs

Cut the carrots and swede into 2-inch sticks of macaroni thickness and simmer till done in water to cover. Then add 1 oz. butter and a tablespoon brown sugar for each 3 cups of vegetables and toss over heat till caramelized. Cut jacket cooked potatoes into thick slices and sauté 5 minutes in butter. For the Fritters, slice and fry the onions, when lightly browned, add the sliced tomatoes and cook together 5 minutes more, pour in the beaten, seasoned eggs, cook over good heat till the eggs are set, divide into fritters. Dish all the items on a hot platter and serve hot.

MACARONI, SPAGHETTI, Etc.

Macaroni, Mushroom and Egg Savoury

4 oz. macaroni	1 tablespoon grated onion
4 oz. cooked mushrooms	1 cup soft bread crumbs
4 oz. grated cheese	½ teaspoon salt
½ pint white sauce	pinch each: pepper and nutmeg
3 eggs	

Boil the macaroni tender and drain. Mince the cooked mushrooms fine and add. Stir in all the remaining ingredients *except* the whites of the eggs. Whip the whites of the eggs to a stiff froth and carefully fold into the mixture. Turn into a well-greased, deep casserole filling it about two-thirds. Bake in a slow oven, Gas Mark 4, or 350 deg., for 45 minutes. Serve hot with tomato sauce and peas or carrots.

Macaroni Ramekins with Vegetables

6 oz. macaroni	6 oz. grated cheese
½ pint hot milk	1 tablespoon minced parsley
1 cup bread crumbs	1 tablespoon minced onion
2 eggs	½ teaspoon salt
2 tablespoons butter	creamed vegetables

Boil the macaroni tender, drain, add hot milk, stir in the beaten eggs and all the other ingredients except the creamed vegetables. Grease several small ramekin moulds and sprinkle with fine bread raspings, then fill with the mixture. Bake in a moderate oven 35 minutes, stand 3 minutes, unmould and dish around the edge of a hot platter. Put the creamed vegetables in the centre. Serve hot. *Note.* Any attractive selection of cooked vegetables suits this dish, e.g. diced carrots, cauliflower sprigs, peas. Simmer 2 cups of cooked vegetables in a cup of creamy White Sauce, stirring gently till hot. The sauce should be made with butter, and have a little cream or top milk stirred in.

Spinach Noodle Pie

½ lb. spinach noodles
2 eggs
seasoning
1 cup fried onions

½ lb. sliced tomatoes
½ pint cheese sauce
butter and bread crumbs

Boil the noodles tender, drain, mix with the well-beaten eggs, seasoned to taste. Put half the mixture in a greased pie dish, cover with a layer of fried onions, sliced tomatoes, moistened with cheese sauce. Repeat once. Sprinkle bread crumbs over, dot with butter. Bake in a moderate oven about 35 minutes.

Note. Spinach noodles are ribbon macaroni containing spinach which is mixed with the dough during manufacture. The resulting product is of a delicate green tint and agreeable flavour. Most Italian stores sell it at popular prices.

Spaghetti with Almond Quenelles

4 oz. spaghetti
3 hard-boiled eggs
1 pint cheese sauce

2 peeled tomatoes
1 cup almond nutmeat mixture

Boil the spaghetti tender, drain, mix gently with the quartered hard-boiled eggs, diced tomatoes and cheese sauce. Turn into a buttered pie dish or shallow casserole, top with small kite-shaped rissoles made of the nutmeat mixture. Bake in a moderate oven ½ hour. Serve hot.

Macaroni with Nutmeat

6 oz. macaroni (large)
½ lb. sliced nutmeat
2 beaten eggs
2 cups fried onion rings

tomato sauce
1 oz. butter
seasoning

Boil the macaroni tender, drain, add the butter and seasoning, simmer and stir 5 minutes, remove from heat, stir in the beaten eggs. Put a layer of the prepared macaroni in a buttered casserole, cover with sliced nutmeat, onion rings, and tomato sauce. Repeat the layers to fill the casserole, bake in a moderate oven ½ hour. *Note.* The best macaroni for this dish is the cut, wide tube variety known as Zitti. Italian stores supply it. (See pp. 30 and 31 for nutmeat recipes.)

Vermicelli Cheese Soufflé

2 oz. vermicelli
3 eggs
1½ cups bread crumbs
4 oz. flaked cheese
4 tablespoons melted butter

¾ pint scalded milk
1 tablespoon minced parsley
1 tablespoon grated onion
1 teaspoon salt

Boil the vermicelli 8 minutes, drain, pour the milk on, add melted butter, parsley and onion, salt, cheese, bread crumbs and the beaten yolks of the eggs. Stir well. Whip the whites of the eggs to a froth and fold in. Pour into a greased casserole or pie dish, cover with a buttered paper, stand dish in a tin of hot water, bake in a moderate oven 1 hour, removing paper after 20 minutes. Note: See p. 104 for Soufflés.

Noodle and Nutmeat Pie

4 oz. noodles (ribbon macaroni)
2 eggs
2 oz. grated cheese
1 tablespoon butter

½ teaspoon salt
grate of nutmeg
½ recipe nutmeat

Boil noodles tender, drain, stir in the beaten eggs and the rest of the ingredients, except nutmeat. Put half the noodle mixture in a buttered pie dish, dot with pellets of nutmeat, sprinkle with salt and nutmeg. Spread the rest of the noodles over, dot with butter. Bake ½ hour in a moderate oven. Serve hot with Tomato Sauce and vegetables. Note: See Nouilles (Egg Noodles) p. 62.

Macaroni Timbales

6 oz. macaroni
2 eggs
2 oz. grated cheese
4 oz. cooked mushrooms

1 tablespoon grated onion
bread raspings
seasoning

Boil macaroni tender, drain well, stir in the cheese, 1 beaten egg and seasoning. Butter 6 small moulds and sprinkle with fine bread raspings. Fill with the macaroni mixture, make a hollow in each. Mix the chopped cooked mushrooms with the remaining beaten egg, and fill the hollows with the mixture. Bake 30 minutes in a moderate oven, stand 3 minutes, unmould on to a hot platter, and pour tomato sauce around. To vary, border the timbales with mixed diced vegetables.

Baked Savoury Macaroni

½ lb. macaroni
½ pint hot milk
½ lb. grated cheese
1 cup fried onions
2 beaten eggs

1 clove garlic (grated)
½ cup minced parsley
1 level teaspoon salt
¼ teaspoon dried thyme
pinch each: pepper and nutmeg

Boil the macaroni tender, drain well, pour in the hot milk, then add the remaining ingredients in the order stated. Mix well, turn into a buttered pie dish keeping the mixture not more than 1 inch deep. Bake in a moderate oven about 45 minutes. Serve hot, with grilled tomatoes and peas or greens. *Note*. See Macaroni Fritters, below.

Macaroni Fritters

Cut cold Baked Savoury Macaroni—recipe above—into wedges, coat in seasoned flour then in beaten egg and fry in shallow, hot fat, turning to brown both sides. Serve hot.

Soho Savoury

6 oz. spaghetti
6 oz. cheese
2 oz. butter
1 bay leaf

1 onion
1 tomato
½ teaspoon salt
grate of nutmeg

Boil the spaghetti with bay leaf and salt until tender, drain, add the butter and cook gently for 5 minutes, stirring. Stir in 4 oz. of grated cheese, grated onion and nutmeg. Spread the spaghetti ½ inch deep in a greased baking tin. Cover with thinly sliced cheese, grate the tomato over the centre, dust nutmeg over, bake in a moderate oven about 20 minutes. Serve hot, cut into squares.

Spaghetti and Tomato Croquettes

6 oz. fine spaghetti
6 oz. grated cheese
1 egg

1 oz. butter
1 cup bread crumbs
salt and pepper to taste

Boil spaghetti, drain well, add the butter and sauté 5 minutes. Stir in the bread crumbs, 4 oz. of the grated cheese, the beaten egg and the seasoning. Let the mixture cool for 1 hour, then deposit 'buns' of it on a buttered baking sheet. Cut the rest of the cheese into little sticks and put one in the top of each croquette. Sprinkle a few bread crumbs over. Bake in a hot oven for 20 minutes. Serve hot with tomato sauce and mixed vegetables.

Italian Spaghetti

½ lb. spaghetti	1 clove garlic
4 oz. mushrooms	3 oz. grated cheese
1 onion	¾ pint vegetable stock
2 tomatoes	olive oil
6 black olives	salt, pepper and nutmeg

Boil the spaghetti tender, drain well. Brown chopped onion in olive oil, add sliced mushrooms and cook 5 minutes more, add stock, sliced tomatoes, grated garlic, sliced olives and simmer 10 minutes. Add seasonings, then the cooked spaghetti and cook 5 minutes over gentle heat. Serve hot with grated cheese sprinkled over at the very last.

Baked Curd Cheese Pudding

4 oz. ribbon macaroni	2 oz. butter
½ lb. fresh curd cheese	pinch of salt and nutmeg
1 egg	

Boil the macaroni tender, cool a little, stir in the beaten egg and seasonings. Butter a small deep casserole and put in a layer of the macaroni mixture, cover with dots of curd cheese, dots of butter and a sprinkling of seasoning. Repeat till the casserole is filled, and let macaroni be the topmost layer. Bake in a moderately hot oven, Gas Mark 5, or 375 deg., for about 45 minutes. Serve hot, cut into wedges. Sour cream is the best adjunct for this dish.

Spaghetti, Corn and Peas

½ lb. spaghetti	2 oz. flaked cheese
2 cups cooked corn off the cob	1 oz. butter
2 cups cooked peas	seasoning
3 hard-boiled eggs	

Break the spaghetti into short lengths, boil, drain, then sauté in the butter 5 minutes. Add the drained peas and corn, the diced hard-boiled eggs and the cheese, with seasoning to taste. Reheat gently, stirring till thoroughly hot. *Note.* The end of the summer is the best time for this dish, for garden peas are still available and corn on the cob is at its best. Alternatively, canned sweet corn is used, provided a good kind can be obtained; and canned peas, of course, are always with us.

Baked Tomato Macaroni

½ lb. large macaroni
6 oz. grated cheese
½ lb. sliced tomatoes
1 grated onion
1 clove garlic, grated

½ cup minced parsley
1 small cup unsweetened, eva-
    porated milk
bread crumbs to sprinkle
seasoning

Boil the broken macaroni till tender, drain, stir in the grated cheese (reserving a little for the top), the onion and garlic, milk, parsley and seasoning, and half the sliced tomatoes. Put the mixture in a buttered baking dish so that its depth is just over an inch, put the rest of the tomatoes on the top, sprinkle cheese and bread crumbs over, dot with fat. Bake in a moderate oven ½ hour. Serve with onion sauce or tomato sauce.

Vermicelli Nut Savouries

½ lb. vermicelli
4 oz. ground almonds or walnuts
1 oz. butter
1 oz. grated cheese

1 egg
1 cup fried onions
seasoning

Boil the vermicelli 7 minutes, drain, stir in the grated cheese, butter, beaten egg and seasoning, then spread half the mixture in a greased shallow baking tin. Mix nuts, fried onions and seasoning, and spread over the vermicelli. Cover with the rest of the vermicelli. Bake in a moderate oven ½ hour. Cut into squares, serve hot with crisply roasted potatoes, peas, and brown gravy.

Macaroni and Vegetable Savoury

½ lb. large macaroni
½ pint rich cheese sauce
¼ lb. each: celery, onions and
    leeks

1 oz. butter
grated cheese and bread crumbs
seasoning

Prepare the vegetables and stew gently with the butter and very little water till tender. Break the macaroni—the large diameter macaroni is best, bought from Italian stores—into short lengths, boil and drain. Chop the cooked vegetables rather fine and mix

gently with the cooked macaroni and the cheese sauce, seasoning
to taste. Turn into a buttered dish, sprinkle cheese and a few bread
crumbs over, dot with butter, brown under the griller. Serve hot.
Note. The cooking liquor drained from the vegetables should be
added to the cheese sauce. When making the Cheese Sauce stir
in the cheese—a generous amount—at the last moment. (See p. 24.
Cheese Sauce.)

Cheese and Spaghetti Rissoles

4 oz. spaghetti
2 eggs
1 cup fried onions
bread crumbs

4 oz. grated cheese
1 dessertspoon flour
pinch of herbs and seasoning
frying fat

Cook the broken spaghetti till tender, drain, mix with the flour,
herbs and seasoning, grated cheese, fried onions and 1 beaten egg.
Spread on a large greased plate and let stand 2 hours. Cut into
wedges, coat in seasoned flour, beaten egg, and then in fine bread
crumbs. Fry in hot fat, turning to cook both sides nut brown.
Chipped potatoes and grilled tomatoes are good with the rissoles.

Macaroni Haricot Hot Pot

4 oz. large macaroni
1 small tin baked beans
1 egg
2 cups cooked leeks and celery

¾ pint rich sauce
bread crumbs
seasoning
butter for dotting

Break the macaroni into short lengths, boil till tender, drain, mix
with beaten egg and seasoning. Put layers of prepared macaroni,
vegetables, baked beans in a greased hot pot dish, moistening each
with the sauce. Repeat once. Sprinkle top with very few bread
crumbs, dot liberally with butter, cover and bake in a moderate
oven for ½ hour. Uncover during the last 5 minutes.

Nouilles (Egg Noodles)

½ lb. plain flour
1 dessertspoon cold water
1 egg

yolk of 1 egg
pinch of salt

Sift flour and salt into a bowl, make a hollow, put in the egg yolk
and water. Mix to a dough, knead for 5 minutes to make smooth
and elastic. Divide the dough into 3 pieces, and roll each into a
sheet, paper thin, on a flour-dusted board.

Hang the rolled sheets of paste carefully on a line covered with a flour-dusted sheet of paper, to dry sufficiently. The dough must not be allowed to become dry and brittle. When, after testing by touch, the sheets of paste seem right for cutting, roll them up loosely—like a very slack Swiss roll—and, with a sharp knife, cut diagonally into strips either ⅛, ¼, or ½ inch wide according to requirements. These are further dried for ½ hour before cooking. The noodles are boiled till tender, in the same way as all the other varieties of Italian paste which, of course, are made of semolina, salt and water, whereas real noodles are made of flour and eggs; many factory-made noodles, however, are made of the usual semolina dough used for macaroni.

The boiled noodles are used in many savoury dishes, and for adding to soups. The sheets of Nouilles paste, before rolling and cutting, are used for making Ravioli; recipe below.

Ravioli

Ravioli are tiny envelopes of Nouilles paste, containing a spot of savoury filling. They are poached in stock or water, or boiled in soups. To prepare them, place a filbert of savoury stuffing at intervals all over a sheet of nouilles paste and cover with another sheet of the paste. With a pastry wheel or similar tool, mark off into squares and cut through to produce the little envelopes. Alternatively, the paste is cut into 2-inch rounds with a biscuit cutter, a dot of stuffing placed on one half of each round, and the Ravioli folded turnover fashion. Spinach purée, well-drained, mixed with plenty of rich, grated cheese, bound with beaten egg yolk, and flavoured with salt, pepper and grated garlic, is a popular Italian Ravioli stuffing. Cook till well done. The cooked Ravioli are sometimes piled on a hot dish, moistened with tomato sauce, sprinkled with grated cheese and browned quickly under the griller.

SAVOURY EGG DISHES

Creamed Eggs and Mushrooms

6 hard-boiled eggs	1 pint white sauce
¼ lb. button mushrooms	½ pint milk
1 teaspoon grated onion	seasoning

Simmer the whole mushrooms in the milk with a pinch of seasoning added, and drain when tender. Add the mushroom liquor to the sauce, add the grated onion, add 1 diced hard-boiled egg and the remaining eggs whole. Simmer 3 or 4 minutes, then add the mushrooms. Serve hot. *Note.* The White Sauce should be rather thick.

Savoury Baked Eggs

6 eggs
about 1 lb. mashed potato
½ pint onion sauce

2 oz. grated cheese
bread crumbs
paprika

Butter a large glass oven dish, sprinkle thickly with bread crumbs, put in a substantial layer of smoothly mashed potato leaving a clear channel around the edge. With the base of a tumbler make 6 hollows in the potato. Put a teaspoon of the Onion Sauce in each, then carefully break an egg into each hollow. Pour the rest of the sauce into the channel and sprinkle the sauce with the grated cheese. Bake in a moderate oven till the eggs are set. Serve hot, sprinkling a pinch of paprika over each portion. *Note.* A little beaten egg is sometimes added to the mashed potato, and the potato edge is piped.

Savoury Fried Eggs

Lightly brown 2 or 3 sliced onions in butter, pile the onions at the side of the pan and sprinkle with grated cheese. Add more butter to the pan and when hot, break in 4 eggs. Cover for 2 minutes while cooking gently, then remove cover and fry till the eggs are done. Pipe a border of mashed potato around the edges of 4 rounds of buttered toast, and put a fried egg with onions in the centre of each. Serve hot. *Note.* The potato may be replaced by buttered, well-cooked noodles, and, to vary, use tomatoes in place of onions. A large pan will be required in either case.

Eggs Au Gratin

Line a buttered baking dish—glass for preference—with thin slices of wholemeal bread and butter, and sprinkle grated cheese on the edge of each slice. Break an egg on to each slice, bake till the eggs set. Spread a little white sauce over the eggs, sprinkle grated cheese over, scatter a few bread crumbs on, return to the oven for 2 minutes. Serve at once.

Egg Curry

6 hard-boiled eggs	1 dessertspoon curry powder
1 lb. onions	¾ pint white sauce
4 oz. butter	6 shreds saffron (see p. 20)

Slice the onions thickly, fry slowly in the butter till pale brown, stir in the curry powder and cook gently together 5 minutes more. Add the white sauce and saffron and simmer 10 minutes. Quarter the hard-boiled eggs, add to the curry, heat gently till thoroughly hot, serve with rice, olives and a salad of celery, apple and onion.

Eggs in Bechamel

Boil the eggs 8 minutes, place under running cold water for a minute, shell, halve, reheat carefully in Bechamel Sauce. Pour into the centre of a piped border of mashed potatoes. Garnish with parsley.

Eggs in Tomatoes

Cut a thin slice from the top (not the stem end) of each tomato, carefully remove the pulp, place on a buttered dish, drop an egg into each cavity. Mix tomato pulp with grated cheese and bread crumbs, season to taste, roll into marbles, place around the tomatoes. Bake till the eggs are set.

Scotch Eggs

Boil the eggs 8 minutes, rinse under cold water, shell. Mould savoury nutmeat mixture around each egg, coat in beaten egg and bread crumbs, fry in deep hot fat. Good hot or cold.

Eggs in Little Dishes

The plain poached egg is enhanced by various additions and a final moment in the oven to finish it. *1.* Put the required number of poached eggs each in a little fireproof China case, put a spoonful of tomato purée on each, add a spoonful of cream, put in the oven for 2 minutes, serve hot. *2.* Put a little parsley sauce in each dish, add a freshly poached egg, sprinkle grated cheese over, brown lightly under the griller. *3*. Half fill the cases with soft bread crumbs flavoured with shredded fresh thyme or marjoram, add a poached egg, top with a spoonful of mushroom sauce, bake 2 minutes. *4*. Half fill the cases with a mixture of fried onion and tomato and cream, add a poached egg, pour a little cheese sauce on, finish under griller. *5*. Put a pat of fresh butter, a teaspoon of minced chives and parsley in the case, add a poached egg, sprinkle grated cheese on, and finally, a teaspoon of grated raw tomato. Finish under the griller. *6*. Half fill the case with Bechamel sauce, add a poached egg, pour on a spoonful of beaten egg blended with the same amount of cream and seasoned with salt and pepper. Bake till the top is lightly set. *Note.* Stir freshly minced parsley into thin White Sauce, for Parsley Sauce, and serve at once. The amount of parsley is a matter of taste.

Mushroom Soufflé

6 oz. mushrooms	2½ oz. flour
3 eggs	½ pint milk
3 oz. butter	pinch each: salt and pepper

Chop the peeled mushrooms fine and brown lightly in the butter, stir in the flour and seasonings, gradually add the milk, stirring constantly until thickened. When cooled, beat in the yolks of the eggs singly. Lastly, whip the whites to a stiff froth and fold in. Pour into a deep, buttered baking dish, and bake 30 minutes in a slow to moderate oven, Gas Mark 4, or 350 deg. Serve immediately. *Note.* See p. 104 for Soufflés.

STUFFINGS AND TOPPINGS

D'Uxelles Stuffing

4 oz. mushrooms	1 oz. butter
4 oz. parsley	seasoning
1 oz. chopped shallot or onion	

Chop shallot or onion, fry gently in the butter 5 minutes. Add the finely chopped mushrooms and fry 5 minutes more. The mixture is now ready for adding to sauces, or mixing with bread crumbs or cooked rice or mashed potato or mashed bread to form savoury stuffings.

Sage and Onion Stuffing

3 onions	a little beaten egg
1 teaspoon dried sage	$\frac{1}{2}$ oz. butter
4 oz. stale bread	salt and pepper to taste

Soak the bread in cold water 10 minutes, press dry, mash smooth. Boil the onions in water till half done, chop fine and mix with the mashed bread. Add sage, butter, seasonings and sufficient beaten egg to bind to a firm paste. Use as required.

Chestnut Stuffing

$\frac{1}{4}$ lb. chestnuts	pinch each: salt, pepper and
$\frac{1}{4}$ lb. bread crumbs	nutmeg
1 oz. butter	$\frac{1}{2}$ beaten egg

Boil the chestnuts, peel, simmer again in a little water till tender, then pound smooth with the bread crumbs, butter, seasonings and the beaten egg.

Banana Stuffing

3 ripe bananas	1 teaspoon butter
1 cup bread crumbs	1 dessertspoon grated cheese

Cream the butter, blend with the mashed bananas, stir in the cheese and bread crumbs. Use for stuffing vegetables, etc.

Rice and Mushroom Stuffing

1 cup cooked rice	1 dessertspoon butter
2 mushrooms	pinch of dried thyme
1 small onion	salt and pepper to taste

Chop the onion fine, brown in the butter, add the minced mushrooms and cook together 3 minutes more. Mix in the cooked rice, herbs and seasonings. Use as required. Good for most stuffed vegetable dishes.

Lentil, Apple and Cheese Stuffing

1 cup cooked lentils	bread crumbs to mix
1 oz. grated cheese	pinch each: pepper, salt and
½ oz. butter	nutmeg
1 cooking apple, baked	

Mash the baked apple, add the cooked lentils, butter and seasonings and blend thoroughly. Add sufficient bread crumbs to form a stiff paste. Good for stuffed vegetables and savouries.

Potato Stuffing

1 cup hot mashed potato	½ teaspoon mixed dried herbs
1 tablespoon fried onion	pinch each: salt, pepper and
1 egg	nutmeg
½ cup bread crumbs	

Beat the egg. Mix with the rest of the ingredients. Use as required.

Bread and Cheese Stuffing

4 oz. grated cheese	½ teaspoon mixed dried herbs
2 cups bread crumbs	pinch each: salt, pepper and
½ oz. butter	nutmeg

Cream the butter, mix with the cheese, stir in the remaining ingredients, mix well. Use for vegetables and savouries.

Vermicelli Topping

2 oz. vermicelli	1 egg
½ pint milk	seasoning
½ oz. butter	

Drop vermicelli into boiling milk, cook 7 minutes. Cool, stir in beaten egg and seasoning. Spread over vegetables and savouries as directed. Dot with butter, bake in a moderate oven.

Savoury Cornflour Topping

$1\frac{1}{2}$ oz. cornflour	$\frac{1}{2}$ pint milk
1 oz. grated cheese	$\frac{1}{2}$ oz. butter

Make a smooth paste of the cornflour with a little of the cold milk, bring the rest of the milk to the boil and pour on, stirring. Cook and stir vigorously over low heat for 2 minutes. Remove from heat, stir in cheese and butter. Stand till firmly set, slice and cover savoury or vegetable dishes, sprinkle grated cheese over, then a few bread crumbs and brown quickly under the griller or in a hot oven. *Note.* This topping may also be used for stuffing certain savoury dishes according to taste.

Rarebit Topping

2 oz. grated cheese	$\frac{1}{4}$ pint milk
1 cup bread crumbs	pinch each: salt, pepper and
$\frac{1}{2}$ oz. butter	nutmeg

Melt butter in a saucepan, stir in the cheese and milk and cook gently till the cheese begins to melt. Add the bread crumbs and seasonings, cook gently 2 minutes more, spread over savouries to be finished in the oven or under the griller till lightly browned.

Cheese and Tomato Topping

Cover the dish with thinly sliced cheese, sprinkle bread raspings over, grate a tomato over the centre, dot with butter, place in the oven till the cheese melts. Use as required to vary baked dishes.

Egg and Tomato Topping

1 cup grated tomato	1 tablespoon grated cheese
3 shredded wheat sections	seasoning
1 egg	

Crush the shredded wheat fine with a rolling pin. Beat the egg. Mix crushed wheat, beaten egg, grated tomato, cheese and seasoning. Use in place of pastry top for savoury pies, and bake in the usual way.

Semolina Cheese Topping

2 oz. semolina	1 egg
½ pint milk	2 tablespoons grated cheese
½ oz. butter	seasoning

Boil milk with butter, sprinkle in the semolina, cook and stir till thickened. Off the heat, stir in the beaten egg, cheese and seasoning. Use as required. Bake in a moderate oven.

Nutmeat and Egg Topping

4 oz. nutmeat	butter for dotting
1 egg	seasoning

Mash the nutmeat smooth, mix in the beaten egg and seasoning. Spread over vegetables or savouries, dot with butter, bake in a moderate oven. Use as required.

LIGHT VEGETABLE SAVOURIES

Haricot Potato Casserole

2 cups cooked haricots, or   1 carrot
1 tin baked beans   1 teaspoon black treacle
2 oz. flaked cheese   1 cup gravy
1 lb. cooked potatoes   seasoning
1 onion

Cut the cooked potatoes into large cubes. Grate the onion and carrot raw. Put a layer of the potatoes in a buttered casserole, sprinkle seasoning, grated carrot and onion over, add flaked cheese, then a layer of cooked beans. Repeat once. Melt the treacle in the hot gravy and pour in. Bake 1 hour in a moderate oven. *Note.* The tastier the gravy, the better the dish; simmer it with a herb bouquet, then add a teaspoon of extract and a grate of nutmeg before adding to the casserole. A good winter dish, this.

Autumn Potato Pie

2 lb. cooked potatoes   1 cup gravy (thickened)
2 onions   seasoning
1 cup cooked peas   frying fat
¼ lb. mushrooms   pastry for top

Slice the onions, fry light brown, add sliced mushrooms and fry 3 minutes more. Put a layer of thickly sliced, cooked potatoes in a greased pie dish, add half the onions and mushrooms, a sprinkling of seasoning, then half the peas. Repeat the filling once, pour in the thickened gravy, cover with thinly rolled pastry, brush with milk or beaten egg, bake till pastry is well browned.

Sweet Potato Hot Pot

1 lb. potatoes   2 oz. butter
½ lb. carrots   1 cup thick sauce
½ lb. swedes   6 small dumplings
½ lb. onions   1 tablespoon treacle

71

Boil carrots and swede tender, then dice swede and chip carrots. Mix both with the *raw* diced potatoes, raw chopped onions, and seasoning. Turn mixture into a buttered casserole. Add dumplings. Stir treacle into sauce and pour in. Put dots of butter on top. Cover. Bake 3 hours in a slow oven, or on a cooking mat.

Egg and Potato Fry

1 lb. cooked potatoes   butter for frying
½ lb. onions   seasoning
3 eggs

Slice onions thick, brown lightly in butter, add thickly sliced potatoes, cook and stir 5 minutes. Beat eggs with seasoning, increase heat, pour in beaten eggs. Lift edges to let fluid egg flow under, cook till eggs set. Serve, unfolded and hot.

Savoury Potato Pudding

3 cups grated raw potato   2 eggs
1 grated raw onion   1 oz. butter
1 tablespoon flour   seasoning

Mix grated raw potato, onion and flour with seasoning to taste, stir in the well-beaten eggs. Melt butter in a baking dish, make hot, pour in potato batter, spread 1 inch deep. Bake in a moderate oven 1¼ hours. Cut into squares, serve hot with Onion Sauce.

Portuguese Onion Savoury

1 lb. button onions   2 tomatoes
1 oz. butter   2 bay leaves
4 oz. cheese   6 peppercorns
4 shreds saffron (optional)   1 clove garlic

Cook onions, minced garlic, butter, bay leaves and peppercorns in a covered casserole, very gently for 2 hours. Lift cover, sprinkle on the snipped saffron, cover with very thinly sliced cheese, grate the tomatoes over, place in a hot oven for 5 minutes, or under the griller till the cheese melts. Fried eggs are good with it.

Cauliflower with Curd Cheese (hors d'œuvre)

1 cooked cauliflower   French dressing (see p. 97)
4 oz. curd cheese   mayonnaise (see p. 25)
3 olives   pinch of paprika

Arrange the flowerlets of cold cooked cauliflower on a dish, sprinkle French dressing over, then spread mayonnaise on the surface. Cream the cheese with very little top milk and a dessertspoon of mayonnaise dressing, and pipe it around the cauliflower, then sprinkle very little paprika on it, here and there. Garnish with sliced olives. Serve cold.

Cauliflower with Mushrooms and Eggs

1 cooked cauliflower   1 cup cheese sauce (see p. 24)
4 oz. mushrooms   butter and grated cheese
2 hard-boiled eggs

Brown mushrooms lightly in butter. Put the sprigs of cooked cauliflower in a buttered fireproof dish, cover with the fried mushrooms, pour the cheese sauce over, sprinkle grated cheese on, reheat in the oven or under the griller.

Curd Cheese Tomato Cups (hors d'œuvre)

Peel, halve, and bake 6 tomatoes in a hot oven for 3 minutes. Cool, remove a little pulp so as to leave cups. Place on a flat dish, put a teaspoon of finely chopped vegetable or mayonnaise in each, blending a little of the removed tomato pulp in the vegetable salad. Pipe around the edge of each tomato cup a ring of curd cheese blended with mayonnaise dressing. Add a pinch of chopped walnut to each curd cheese ring, putting it in one place only. Garnish the platter with diced hard-boiled egg and black olives.

Celeriac with Egg and Cheese Sauce

Peel and scrub some small roots of celeriac, and cut into slices ½ inch thick. Cover with cold water and simmer for ½ hour or till tender. Use the cooking liquid, with milk, to make ½ pint White Sauce, stir in seasoning, 2 oz. grated cheese and gradually stir in the beaten yolk of an egg. Put the cooked celeriac in a buttered baking dish, pour the sauce over, bake 20 minutes in a slow oven.

Asparagus Au Gratin

Scrape ½ bundle asparagus, wash, then tie in smaller bunches with tape. Cut end off stems to make even lengths. Cook in boiling water 10 to 15 minutes, drain and place in a buttered dish. Grate a freshly cooked hard-boiled egg into ½ pint white sauce and pour over the asparagus. Sprinkle with cheese and bread crumbs, dot with butter, brown under the griller, or in a quick oven.

Asparagus with Poached Eggs

Cook the asparagus as in the previous recipe, place in a fireproof dish, sprinkle flaked cheese over, dot thickly with butter, bake 5 minutes in a hot oven. Serve with trimmed, poached eggs and pats of parsley butter.

Nut Stuffed Mushrooms

4 large mushrooms	seasoning
2 onions	grated cheese
1 oz. ground almonds or walnuts	oil and lemon juice
1 tablespoon minced parsley	frying fat

Score the mushroom caps and grill, or bake on a greased tin. Grate 2 teaspoons of raw onion, chop the rest of the onions fine and fry 3 minutes, add the chopped mushroom stalks, parsley and nuts, and fry 2 minutes more. Sprinkle seasoning, oil and lemon juice into the grilled mushroom caps, fill with the onion mixture, top with grated raw onion, then with grated cheese. Place under griller for 3 minutes. Serve on toast, or in a border of mashed potatoes, or with fried eggs.

Egg and Mushroom Savoury

½ lb. mushrooms	grated raw onion
4 eggs	½ oz. butter
grated cheese	pepper and salt

Slice mushrooms, stew in butter, put in a shallow oven dish. Break the eggs on to the mushrooms. Sprinkle grated onion, then seasoning, then grated cheese over. Bake till eggs are set. Then, for a toasted finish, brown a little more under the griller.

Button Mushroom and Egg Flan

4 oz. button mushrooms	short crust pastry
3 hard-boiled eggs	grated cheese
1 cup white sauce	seasoning

Line a flan ring or Victoria sandwich tin with the thinly-rolled pastry. Stew the mushrooms with the butter, seasoning and very little milk, cool them and turn into the pastry-lined tin. Add the sliced hard-boiled eggs, pour in the sauce, sprinkle grated cheese over, bake till pastry is done.

Savoury Stuffed Marrows

1 medium size young marrow	1 cup bread crumbs
4 oz. flaked cheese	grate of nutmeg
1 egg	seasoning
1 onion	butter for dotting
2 tomatoes	

Simmer whole marrow till tender, cool, peel, cut into thick rings, put half of them in a well-buttered pie dish. Mix the grated raw onion, grated tomatoes, bread crumbs, flaked cheese, nutmeg and seasoning and spread half the mixture over the marrow in the dish. Cover with the rest of the marrow rings, top with the rest of the stuffing mixture. Dot with butter. Bake 35 minutes in a moderate oven.

Ragoût of Baby Marrows

6 four-inch marrows	$\frac{1}{2}$ pint Bechamel sauce (see p. 22)
4 oz. mushrooms	
2 onions	seasoning
1 teaspoon yeast extract	butter for frying

Slice onions thickly and brown lightly in the butter, add sliced mushrooms and cook together 5 minutes more. Wipe baby marrows, simmer whole till tender, then slice thickly; do not peel. Put cooked marrows and mushroom-onion mixture in a casserole, pour in the sauce with extract dissolved in it. Reheat gently till thoroughly hot.

Aubergines Stuffed and Baked

4 small aubergines
½ lb. onions
2 tomatoes
½ cup boiled rice

1 clove garlic
grated cheese
seasoning
frying fat

Boil the unpeeled aubergines 5 minutes, cool, halve lengthwise and remove a little of the pulp to leave thick shells. Brown chopped onions in fat, add the diced peeled tomatoes, grated garlic and the chopped aubergine pulp, and cook gently together 4 or 5 minutes more; mix with the rice, pile the mixture into the aubergine shells, bake on a buttered dish, in a moderate oven, for 35 minutes.

Aubergine and Tomato Savoury

2 aubergines
4 tomatoes
1 onion
2 oz. grated cheese

olive oil
flour
seasoning

Thinly peel aubergines, slice ¼ inch thick, sprinkle flour over, fry gently in oil for 3 minutes, drain. Lightly brown chopped onions, add peeled sliced tomatoes and cook 3 minutes more. Put half the fried aubergine slices in a greased pie dish, add a layer consisting of seasoning and tomato-onion mixture, and half the grated cheese. Cover with the rest of the aubergines, top with the rest of the grated cheese. Bake 20 minutes in a moderately hot oven, Gas Mark 5 or 375 deg.

Egg and Spinach Ramekins

Wash 1 lb. spinach, cook rapidly in very little more water than adheres to the leaves after washing, drain, add a large pat of butter and cook gently 2 minutes more. Stir in a beaten egg, 1 oz. grated cheese, pepper and salt, and a grate of nutmeg. Pack into small, buttered ramekin dishes and bake 15 minutes in a moderate oven.

Swedes Baked in Butter

Pare 1½ lb. of yellow swede and cut into walnut size chunks, simmer in water to cover, and when tender, drain and turn into a well buttered oven dish. Add a few forcemeat balls, dot with butter, bake in a moderate oven ½ hour. Sprinkle a little minced parsley over before serving, and yet more dots of butter. A simple dish, but an attractive one. *Note.* Forcemeat balls of the tastiest kind are made by rolling leftovers of any savoury into marbles, adding bread crumbs if required for consistency.

Baked Artichoke Savoury

2 lb. Jerusalem artichokes	2 eggs
1 dessertspoon grated onion	2 oz. ground cashew nuts
¼ pint thick sauce	grate of nutmeg, pepper and salt

Wash, peel, slice the artichokes thickly, cover with cold water, simmer till tender (about 15 minutes). Drain, mash smooth, mix with ground nuts, grated onion, beaten eggs, seasonings and sauce. Turn into a buttered dish, bake in a moderate oven just under 1 hour. Serve with cheese sauce and grilled tomatoes.

Globe Artichoke Fritters

Only the bottoms of the young artichokes are used for this dish. To prepare these, cut the leaves down to level with the top of the base, using sharp scissors. Trim the sides and base, and boil the resulting discs (' artichoke bottoms ') for 5 minutes. Drain well, coat in seasoned flour, then in beaten eggs or in frying batter and fry in deep hot fat till golden brown. Serve hot.

Stuffed Cabbage Rolls

1 small cabbage	2 tomatoes
1 cup cooked rice	rich brown gravy
1 oz. ground almonds	butter
1 cup fried onions	seasoning

Boil the cabbage rapidly in covered pan 7 minutes, drain, cool, separate several of the tender leaves and lay them on a pastry board. Mix rice, almonds, fried onions, diced peeled tomatoes and seasoning, and put a spoonful on each leaf. Roll up the stuffed leaves and tie with white thread. Place in a dish containing gravy ½ inch deep. Cook gently ½ hour. Place a pat of butter on each roll before serving. *Note.* Grated cheese may replace ground almonds for variation.

Cabbage Au Gratin

Separate the leaves of a small boiled cabbage, drain, place on a buttered fireproof dish. Sprinkle with flaked cheese, a little grated onion and a pinch of nutmeg, lifting the inner leaves to make sure they all receive the dressing. Sprinkle a few bread crumbs over, dot very generously with butter, put the dish in a hot oven for 5 minutes.

Red Cabbage with Sour Cream

1 fresh red cabbage	juice of 1 lemon
1 onion	2 oz. butter
2 oz. seedless raisins	pinch salt
2 tablespoons chopped onion	4 tablespoons sour cream

Shred cabbage fine, rinse under cold water, mix with onion, raisins, salt, butter, lemon juice and ½ cup cold water. Cook in a covered casserole over low heat for 2½ hours, adding a little more water if required at half stage. Serve with a dressing of sour cream.

Carrots in Mushroom Sauce

Simmer ¾ lb. chipped carrots till tender. Add 2 oz. fried, minced mushrooms to ¾ pint white sauce, add a herb bouquet, add cooked carrots. Simmer 20 minutes. Before serving, stir in a walnut of butter, a squeeze of lemon and a pinch of grated nutmeg.

Sweet Corn, Peas and Vermicelli

Remove husks and silk from 7 or 8 cobs of corn, and with a sharp knife remove the kernels. Simmer the kernels in milk about 10 minutes or till tender. Add a cup of cooked peas, and a cup of cooked vermicelli. Reheat and add a pat of butter before serving.

Egg and Beet Savoury

2 cups diced boiled beets	grated cheese
1 cup fried chopped onions	mashed potatoes
2 hard-boiled eggs	seasoning
lemon juice	

Add the diced beets to the fried onions, cook together 2 or 3 minutes. Stir in the lemon juice, seasoning and the chopped, hard-boiled eggs and turn into a buttered oven dish. Pipe a border of mashed potato around, sprinkle potato with grated cheese, bake 15 minutes in a hot oven.

Beetroot and Potato Fritters

Put thick slices of boiled beets in oil and lemon dressing and stand 20 minutes. Coat the marinaded beet slices with flour, cover each slice with mashed potato, coat in good batter, fry in deep hot fat, drain and serve hot with onion salad.

Pea and Potato Croquettes

Mix 1 cup cooked peas, 2 cups mashed potatoes, 1 tablespoon grated onion, 1 beaten egg, ½ cup bread crumbs, seasoning, 1 teaspoon dried mint. Shape the mixture into small balls, bake on a well-buttered tin in a moderately hot oven till tinted. Serve hot.

Sweet Peppers with Noodles

Cut 3 peppers—red, green, or yellow, into ¼-inch rings. Simmer in water to cover till tender, drain, toss in butter with a little chopped onion, adding 2 sliced peeled tomatoes towards the end. Dish on a bed of noodles; these are best when drained after boiling, then fried for a few minutes in butter.

Stuffed Sweet Peppers

Simmer the entire peppers in water to cover for 12 minutes. Cool, halve, remove seeds, fill with a tasty stuffing (see p. 68), place on a buttered baking dish, put tomato halves in the odd corners, bake 45 minutes in a moderate oven. Add a little gravy to the tin after the first 2 minutes.

Note 1. For Cheese Stuffing, mix a beaten egg with 1 cup cooked rice, 1 cup flaked cheese, 1 cup bread crumbs and no seasoning as the peppers tend to taste 'hot' in any case, and the cheese contains salt. *2.* Small peppers simmered as described above, cooled, cut into long halves, freed from seeds, and filled with Russian Salad bound with Mayonnaise, or cream cheese mixed with diced pickled cucumber, or finely chopped hard-boiled egg blended with thick Mayonnaise, make attractive hors d'œuvre items.

Broad Beans (Oriental)

1 pint cooked, young broad beans	4 dates
2 bananas	2 onions
	butter

Thickly slice and fry the onions slowly in butter and when light brown add the sliced bananas and chopped dates and cook together 3 minutes. Mix in the freshly cooked broad beans and make very hot. Serve with boiled rice and dry toast.

Broccoli, Mushroom and Tomato Pie

1 lb. broccoli	1 cup cheese sauce
4 oz. mushrooms	short crust pastry
2 tomatoes	

Prepare and boil the broccoli 20 minutes or till tender, drain, divide into flowerlets, and finely slice stems. Meanwhile, brown the sliced mushrooms in butter. Peel and dice the tomatoes. Turn the cooked broccoli, mushrooms and tomatoes into a buttered pie dish, pour in the sauce, cover with thinly rolled pastry, brush with milk or beaten egg. Bake till pastry is well done. Serve hot.

Broccoli Fritters

Drain cooked broccoli, divide into flowerlets, dip in seasoned flour then coat in rich frying batter, and fry in hot fat or oil. Drain, sprinkle grated cheese over. Serve with mashed potatoes.

Boletus (Edible Fungi)

Boletus, usually found in the vicinity of beech and birch trees during the autumn, is notably good in soups and stews. Sliced, and fried in butter it is a delectable garnishing vegetable to serve with fried or poached eggs, and it partners particularly well with potatoes. With fried onions and tomatoes it is delicious on toast or as an omelet filling. Butter brings out its flavour. Dried boletus is sold by some Italian stores.

Tomato Rarebit

Sprinkle 6 halved tomatoes with oil and lemon, then with grated raw onion and bake lightly for 5 minutes. Take from oven, spread Rarebit mixture on them, sprinkle with cheese and a few fine breadcrumbs, dot with butter, brown quickly under the griller. Serve on rounds of hot buttered toast. (See Rarebit Topping, p. 69.)

Baked Stuffed Tomatoes

6 tomatoes   seasoning and mace
oil and lemon dressing   butter for dotting

For the stuffing:

½ cup flaked cheese   ½ cup cooked rice
½ cup bread crumbs   1 small egg

Bake the tomatoes lightly, cool, halve, remove a little of the pulp, leaving cups. Mix the stuffing ingredients, beating the egg slightly before mixing in, and adding seasoning. Sprinkle dressing in the tomato cups, dust with mace and seasoning, pile in the filling, dot with butter, bake in a quick oven 6 minutes. Serve with crusty rolls or crisp toast.

Tomato Sauté

¾ lb. tomatoes   ½ pint white sauce
¼ lb. button mushrooms   ¼ pint tomato purée
3 hard-boiled eggs   ½ oz. butter
seasoning   1 herb bouquet

Stew prepared mushrooms tender, with butter, herbs and seasoning. Halve the tomatoes and grill them lightly. Quarter the hard-boiled eggs. Put the stewed mushrooms, grilled tomatoes, and quartered hard-boiled eggs on a buttered dish. Cover with blended white sauce and tomato purée. Reheat and serve hot. *Note.* Capers, cocktail onions, or diced gherkins may be added to the sauté as wished.

Onions with Puff Balls

Fry 1 lb. thickly sliced onions in butter very slowly in a pan covered part of the time, till nut brown. Add 2 cups sliced, freshly gathered puff balls, cook gently together for 5 minutes, uncovered, and stirring now and then. Serve hot on toast, sprinkled with freshly ground black pepper. An exceptionally delicious dish.

Onion and Potato Flan

1 lb. mashed potatoes   4 large onions
1 tablespoon flour   2 eggs
1½ oz. butter   grated cheese to sprinkle

Stew the diced onions with the butter and a little water till very tender. Do not drain. Cool a little, then stir in one of the beaten eggs, duly seasoned. Now stir flour into the dry, mashed potato, add seasoning and the remaining beaten egg, and spread this potato mixture thickly in a buttered pie dish. Fill with the onion mixture. Bake in a moderate oven for ½ hour. Serve hot. Tomato sauce is good with it.

Cauliflower with Spinach Noodles

1 cauliflower	2 oz. butter
4 oz. spinach noodles	1 cup cheese sauce
grated cheese	bread crumbs

Boil the cauliflower tender, drain well, divide into flowerlets, put evenly in a buttered baking dish. The noodles are boiled separately while the cauliflower cooks; drain them well, put them in a pan with the butter, sauté 5 minutes, then place them around the cauliflower as a border. Pour the sauce over the cauliflower. Sprinkle with grated cheese, then with bread crumbs. Brown quickly in a hot oven or under the griller. *Note.* If spinach noodles are not available (Italian stores sell them cheaply) use plain noodles —these are narrow ribbon macaroni.

Chanterelle (Edible Fungi)

The yellow, trumpet shaped fungus, found in forest areas during the autumn, requires a few minutes simmering to make it tender. It is then tossed in butter for a few minutes, or fried with onions and tomatoes, or drained, coated in batter and cooked in hot fat for delicious fritters. Mixed with sliced boletus (see recipe, p. 80) it is appetizing in vegetable soups. Sliced puff balls partner well with it in vegetable stews.

Leek and Lentil Savoury

1 lb. young leeks	4 oz. lentils
1 oz. butter	1 egg
1 oz. grated cheese	1 bay leaf
butter for dotting	seasoning

Trim the leeks, retaining 2 inches of the green, simmer with a little water and butter till tender. Simmer lentils with a bay leaf in water to cover for 25 minutes, mix with beaten egg, grated cheese and seasoning. Put leeks in a buttered pie dish, cover with the lentil mixture, dot with butter, bake ½ hour in a moderate oven.

Leek and Tomato Savoury

Sauté sliced young leeks till lightly coloured, add an equal amount of peeled tomatoes, seasoning and a little more butter, and put in a pie dish. Sprinkle thickly with grated cheese, scatter a few bread crumbs over, dot with butter, bake in a moderately hot oven about ½ hour.

Buttered Parsnips

Wash, scrape and slice lengthwise a few young parsnips, barely cover with water, simmer till tender (about ½ hour). Drain, coat in seasoned flour, fry in hot melted butter till browned. Older parsnips take a little longer to cook, but it is the butter that counts.

Peas with Mushrooms and Cheese

Fry 4 oz. sliced mushrooms in butter, mix with a coffee cup of small dice of cheese, add 2 cups drained cooked peas. Cook gently together for 3 minutes, stirring. Just before serving, stir in ½ cup cream.

Pumpkin Savoury

Cut 1½ lb. peeled pumpkin into chunks, simmer till tender, drain, coat first with seasoned flour then with rich batter, pack closely together in a sauté pan containing hot melted butter, pour a little extra batter over, fry golden brown on both sides. Dish up, not as separate fritters, but as a round cake.

Runner Beans in Egg Sauce

Slice young runner beans lengthwise, boil rapidly till tender, drain. Add a finely chopped hard-boiled egg and a teaspoon of lemon juice. Stir the beaten yolk of an egg gradually into ¾ pint white sauce, pour the sauce over the bean and egg mixture, reheat gently but do not let the sauce boil.

STEWS AND RAGOÛTS

Marrow and Mushroom Ragoût

1 medium marrow	2 oz. butter
½ lb. field mushrooms	pinch each: pepper, salt and
2 tomatoes	nutmeg
½ lb. onions	

Boil the marrow whole, cool, peel, cut into chunks. Fry the chopped onions slowly in the butter for 10 minutes, add the sliced mushrooms and cook 5 minutes more, then turn into a greased casserole. Add the cooked marrow with ½ cup of its cooking water, add the fried onions and mushrooms, add the sliced tomatoes and seasoning. A little gravy browning may be added for a rich brown stew. Cook gently 1 hour. Mashed potatoes are good with it.

Winter Casserole

½ lb. potatoes	2 oz. soaked barley
¼ lb. celery	2 cups cooked beans
½ lb. onions	1 oz. butter
1 large carrot	seasoning
¼ lb. tomatoes	

Boil the potatoes, carrot, celery and onions together for ½ hour, drain, and turn into a greased casserole. Add the cooked beans, soaked barley, diced peeled tomatoes, seasoning and 1 cup of the vegetable cooking water. *Note 1.* Add a little more of the cooking water at half stage if necessary to keep the casserole moist. *2.* To vary: stick one of the onions with 6 cloves and add 2 bay leaves and 6 peppercorns; this gives a spicy dish. A cup of cooked macaroni or rice may replace the barley.

Vegetable Casserole with Almond Dumplings

2 cups mixed cooked vegetables	¾ pint Bechamel sauce (see p.
1 cup cooked peas	22)
1 small cooked cauliflower	Almond Dumplings (see under
2 cups boiled onions	'Soup Garnishes', p. 19)

Put all the mixed cooked vegetables, peas, onions and cauliflower in a buttered casserole, pour in the sauce, cook gently 10 minutes, add the Almond Dumplings and cook 15 minutes more. Serve hot.

Summer Vegetable Casserole

¼ lb. mushrooms	2 oz. butter
½ lb. button onions	1 herb bouquet
1 cup garden peas	½ cup cream
1 lb. small new potatoes	½ teaspoon yeast extract
¼ lb. new carrots	seasoning

Melt the butter in a frying pan, add the onions and sliced mushrooms and cook gently 5 minutes. Turn into the casserole, add the rest of the prepared vegetables, the herb bouquet, seasoning and ½ cup boiling water with the extract dissolved in it. Cook gently 1 hour. Remove herbs, stir in cream.

Aubergine and Cauliflower Ragoût

1 cooked cauliflower	2 tomatoes
1 aubergine (medium)	butter or margarine
½ lb. onions	seasoning

Chop the onions, peel and cut the aubergine into small dices, fry both together 10 minutes, add the sliced peeled tomatoes, and cook 5 minutes more. Put the cooked onion-aubergine-tomato mixture in the casserole, add the divided cooked cauliflower, pour in ½ cup boiling water with seasoning in it, cook gently ½ hour. Serve on rounds of buttered toast.

Summer Vegetable Stew

1 cup broad beans	1 cup diced cucumber
1 cup broken French beans	1 herb bouquet
1 cup tiny carrots	yeast extract and seasoning
2 cups peas	butter for frying
2 cups spring onion bulbs	

Lightly brown the chopped spring onion bulbs in butter then turn into the casserole. Add the rest of the prepared vegetables, herbs and seasonings. Dissolve a teaspoon of yeast extract in a cup of boiling water and pour in. Stew gently 1 hour. Serve hot with grated cheese and toasted rolls.

POTATO COOKERY

Mashed Potatoes

Drain the boiled potatoes, dry off a little, mash very smooth with a little butter, while the pan is kept on gentle heat. Then, add a very little hot milk, and, if the potatoes were peeled before cooking, a little of the cooking water and mash again, over gentle heat. It may seem odd to add liquid after the potatoes have been dried, but the drying produces an attractive mealiness which the later addition of a little liquid does not diminish.

Creamed Potatoes

Dice or thickly slice cold boiled potatoes and warm gently in a little thin white sauce. When hot, remove from heat, and stir in cream or top milk.

Hashed Brown Potatoes

Dice jacket-boiled potatoes to sugar cube size, add to each pound of potatoes a finely minced onion and a little seasoning. Press compactly in a thickly buttered frying pan and cook gently to brown the under surface. Sprinkle very little grated cheese on the top and brown the top surface gently under the griller. Lift carefully with a slice on to a hot platter.

Sauté Potatoes

Boil potatoes in their skins, cool, peel, slice thickly. Toss in hot butter over gentle heat till delicately browned. Serve hot.

Pommes Eva

Lightly brown 3 thinly sliced onions in butter. Peel 2 lb. freshly boiled 'jacket' potatoes and put half of them in a buttered casserole. Add half the fried onions, next, add the rest of the potatoes, top with the remaining fried onions, grate an ounce of cheese over, dot with butter, cover, bake ½ hour in a moderate oven. *Note.* Small potatoes should be left whole. Larger ones are best cut into sections.

Sicilian Potatoes

Mash 2 lb. freshly boiled potatoes with a dessertspoon grated onion, a tablespoon of chopped parsley and a grate of garlic. Stir in 2 well-beaten eggs. Spread in a pie dish containing 2 oz. very hot melted butter. Bake 15 minutes in a hot oven.

Potato Chowder

Thinly peel 2 lb. potatoes cut into quarters and put in the soup pan with 6 small onions and a bay leaf. Cover with milk and water. add salt and pepper to taste, but the less salt the better. Bring to the boil, simmer very gently 1½ hours. Stir in ½ cup chopped cress just before serving. Serve very hot, with grated cheese and crusty rolls.

Baked Potatoes

Scrub even-sized potatoes spotlessly clean, put in a moderately hot oven, bake about 1 hour, pierce with a fork, put back in the oven for 10 minutes. Cooking time varies with different kinds of potatoes. To vary the dish, slit open the baked potatoes, and insert a pat of butter and a small tile of cheese.

Boiled Potatoes

Potatoes are best boiled in their skins. Whether started in hot or cold water, potatoes grown in a certain way begin to burst before they are done, to the embarrassment of the cook and the disappointment of the diner. To remedy this, let the potatoes boil gently for about 20 minutes, drain, cover with a fresh teacloth, put on a tight fitting lid, stand pan on a cooking mat and let warm over very gentle heat for 15 minutes, when they will be nicely done, and mealy. Potatoes peeled before cooking often 'burst' too soon, but respond to the same remedy.

Pommes Anna

Cut raw potatoes into thin, even slices. Arrange them in layers in a buttered casserole so that the slices overlap each other, and dot each layer thickly with pellets of butter. Tightly close the dish and bake in a quick oven about ¾ hour.

Maitre D'Hotel Potatoes

Slice 1 lb. boiled new potatoes, or firm old potatoes, into a pan containing a little thin White Sauce, some chopped parsley, and 2 oz. butter. Shake the pan over moderate heat until the ingredients are well blended. Add a sprinkling of lemon juice, and serve hot.

Lyonnaise Potatoes

Brown a chopped onion in butter, add a pound of sliced, boiled new potatoes and cook and stir together for 5 minutes. Scatter a little parsley and salt over and serve immediately.

Casseroled Potatoes

Put 1 oz. butter and 3 tablespoons clear brown gravy in a casserole, add a bunch of parsley, thyme and bay leaf, 6 peppercorns and an onion stuck with 6 cloves. Add 2 lb. even-sized raw potatoes, and bake gently 3 hours. Alternatively, the dish may be cooked gently on an asbestos cooking mat over low heat.

Parisian Potatoes

Generally, these are sliced, cooked potatoes, gently heated in rich onion sauce.

Duchess Potatoes

1 lb. boiled potatoes   pinch each: salt, pepper and
½ oz. butter   nutmeg
yolks of 2 eggs

Pass the peeled, cooked potatoes through a sieve, stir in the butter and seasonings, cook and stir over moderate heat for 2 minutes. Cool a little, stir in the beaten yolks of eggs, cover with a greased paper and let cool. On a floured board, shape into little balls, cottage loaves, miniature French loaves and so on. Brush with beaten egg, place on a greased tin, bake 7 minutes in a hot oven. The potato paste may also be put in a forcing bag and piped through a large star tube into rings, whirls, and 'eclairs'. In the same way a potato border is piped around the edge of a dish containing creamed vegetables, or savouries in sauce, browning in a hot oven as directed. The Duchess Potato paste may also be shaped as croquettes and fried in deep hot fat.

Potato Blinsies

Grate 1 lb. of thinly peeled *raw* potatoes on an old fashioned tin grater (*not* on a modern shredding grater) into a wet mush. Stir in 2 tablespoons plain flour and a teaspoon grated raw onion. Drop tablespoons of the batter into a frying pan containing a good depth of hot frying oil. Level each cake with the back of the spoon. Fry gently, turn the cakes to brown both sides, lift with a slice, drain, serve hot. Sometimes a pinch of salt is sprinkled over the Blinsies, sometimes a pinch of sugar. They are curiously good either way. *Note.* Leave space between the Blinsies as they are dropped on to the pan, as they spread a little in the cooking. Old potatoes are best.

Chipped Potatoes

Thinly peel old potatoes, cut them into slices ½ inch thick, then into even sticks. Dry the chips well on a clean teacloth. Drop them gently into a pan of hot cooking oil, and fry, stirring now and then until nut brown on all sides. Taste one of the chips to make sure they are tender. Drain, and serve immediately. *Note.* A piece of onion in the pan while the chips are cooking adds to their delicacy.

SALADS

Green Salads

Crisp cos lettuce, well washed and dried is good with many hot, savoury dishes, as well as with simple meals of home made bread, butter and cheese. As much may be said of a mixed green salad consisting of lettuce and cress, with a flavouring of chopped spring onions, minced parsley and shredded mint; dress first with lemon juice, then with olive oil. Cucumber is usually a popular addition to most green salads.

In winter, watercress, heart of cabbage, celery tops, endive and parsley are available for green salads which, with the usual accompaniments and garnishes form a relish for many savoury dishes.

Jellied Salads

Pour a film of neutral agar jelly (see p. 147) into several small moulds, and when almost set, loosely fill with diced hard-boiled egg and ingredients selected from the following: asparagus tips, cooked carrot, cauliflower, sliced French beans, peas, tomatoes. The neat dicing of vegetables which need cutting up is important. Pour more jelly into the filled moulds, filling them to the very brim. Chill, unmould, and serve with green salads and savouries. Egg cups as moulds provide attractive garnishing jellies for various dishes.

Dried Fruits for Salads

Raisins, currants, figs, prunes, dried apricots and peaches, and dried bananas are compatible ingredients for many mixed salads. They blend well with most vegetables, cooked or raw, with green leaf salad materials, with tomatoes and cheese of most kinds. Vine fruits such as currants and raisins should be thoroughly washed in hot water and rinsed in cold. The larger dried fruits such as prunes and apricots, figs and peaches, are best soaked for 7 or 8 hours (not cooked) and sliced before adding. They should be used sparingly in mixed salads.

Egg and Potato Salad

Mix 1 lb. diced, freshly cooked potatoes with 2 diced hard-boiled eggs, 1 tablespoon chopped shallot and 1 level teaspoon celery seeds. Toss, first with Oil and Lemon Dressing, then with Mayonnaise. (See Mayonnaise Sauce, p. 25.)

Bobi Indi's Summer Salad

Into a bowl of thick sour cream drop sliced fresh cucumber, trimmed radishes, chopped spring onions, and quartered hard-boiled eggs. The sour cream in this salad is a sauce rather than a dressing, and there can hardly be too much of it. The salad is best eaten with a delicate wooden spoon.

Orange, Grapefruit and Banana Salad

Dice 1 orange and 1 grapefruit, carefully removing pith, membrane and pips. Mix with 4 sliced bananas and equal parts cream, liquid honey and Mayonnaise.

Apple, Pear and Raisin Salad (Winter)

Pour a cup of boiling water over 4 oz. cleaned seedless raisins, stand 12 hours, drain, and mix with 2 cups sliced pears and 1 cup diced sweet apples. Dress with a blend of mayonnaise and liquid honey. Garnish with cress.

Summer Fruit Salad

Mix 1 cup each: sliced strawberries, pitted cherries, ripe black currants and sliced bananas. Stir lemon juice in and pile whipped sour cream on the top. Serve cold.

Russian Salad

A popular English version of this consists of a mixture of 1 cup each: small dice of cooked carrot, white turnip, sliced French beans and peas, dressed with oil and lemon, or with thin mayonnaise. Pickled, or naturally soured cucumber is an agreeable, and perhaps an 'official', addition.

Fruit and Vegetable Salad (1)

1 cup diced tomatoes	1 cup diced apples
1 cup diced cucumber	1 cup diced pears
½ cup sliced gherkins	1 cup diced grapefruit
crisp green lettuce	oil and lemon dressing

Line the salad bowl with the washed and well-dried lettuce. Mix the other ingredients with sufficient dressing to coat them and turn into the bowl. Chill slightly before serving.

Fruit and Vegetable Salad (2)

1 cup chopped watercress	1 cup seedless raisins
1 cup diced tomatoes	1 cup peeled and seeded grapes
1 cup sliced celery	1 cup diced orange
1 cup finely shredded cabbage	French dressing
2 hard-boiled eggs	salad cream
1 cup diced avocado	

Put the ingredients, excepting the eggs, in the salad bowl and mix thoroughly. Spread salad cream on the surface, and top with sliced hard-boiled eggs.

Cooked Vegetable Salad (1)

1 cup cooked cauliflower	2 hard-boiled eggs
1 cup cooked peas	oil and lemon dressing
1 cup diced cooked carrots	flaked cheese
1 cup sliced cooked celery	

Excepting the cheese, put all the ingredients in the prepared salad bowl and toss well. Make a substantial border of flaked cheese. *Note.* To prepare the salad bowl, rub well with a piece of cut garlic.

Cooked Vegetable Salad (2)

1 cup cooked peas	1 cup diced cooked beets
1 cup diced cooked potatoes	2 hard-boiled eggs, diced
1 cup casseroled button onions	mayonnaise dressing

Reserve the beets and 1 of the eggs. Mix the remaining ingredients and put in the bowl. Border with a ring of beets. Garnish with the remaining egg.

Salmagundi

sliced hard-boiled eggs
diced cooked beets
sliced cold nut savoury (see p. 31)
sprigs of cooked cauliflower

diced cooked carrot
sliced celery heart
diced Spanish onion
sliced apple

Put concentric rings of the ingredients on individual plates. Serve with French dressing, thick sour cream, rye bread and pats of butter. *Note.* Summer-time versions of this attractive medley include cucumber, radishes, spring onions, tomatoes, new potatoes, cooked broad beans, and even strawberries.

Spring Salad

sliced tomatoes
trimmed radishes
crisp lettuce
chopped spring onions

diced cucumber
hard-boiled eggs
mayonnaise

Excepting the eggs and lettuce, mix all the ingredients hotch potch fashion and turn them into a garlic-rubbed and lettuce-lined bowl. Cut the eggs, plentiful in the spring, into quarters, and put them in the centre. Crusty rolls and butter should be served.

Winter Salad

1 cup sliced celery heart
1 cup diced cooked potato
1 cup shredded raw cabbage
½ cup grated raw carrot
½ cup diced Spanish onion

½ cup seedless raisins
olive oil
watercress
black olives
lemon cream dressing

Keep the watercress, olives and lemon cream dressing apart. Mix all the remaining ingredients, using the olive oil lavishly. Turn into a prepared salad bowl. Pile the Lemon Cream on top. Garnish with sliced olives and cress. *Note.* For the Lemon Cream, stir 2 tablespoons lemon juice into a cup of unsweetened evaporated milk. Some milks are not as thick as others and may require a little more lemon juice.

Green Peppers with Cream Cheese

Cut out the stem end of the peppers, remove pips, stuff with cream cheese or curd cheese blended with mayonnaise. Chill well, cut into slices, dish up with a garnish of sliced tomatoes.

Potato Salad (1)

Cut freshly peeled 'jacket' potatoes into cubes, and while still warm toss, first, in lemon juice, then in sour cream, adding at the last, a pinch of salt and pepper and carraway seeds or celery seeds.

Potato Salad (2)

Slice freshly cooked potatoes, and while still warm, mix with a flavouring of chopped onion and toss in French dressing. Dish in a bowl rubbed with a cut clove of garlic.

Potato Salad (3)

Mix 2 lb. sliced, freshly cooked potatoes with a tablespoon each of minced parsley, chopped chives, chopped capers, thick mayonnaise dressing, and a pinch of salt and pepper, and a grate of nutmeg.

Cole Slaw

4 cups finely shredded crisp cabbage (raw)	1 teaspoon chopped capers
	French dressing
½ cup diced pickled cucumber	sour cream
¼ cup finely minced onion	pinch of salt

Mix all the ingredients with the French dressing and seasoning, turn into a bowl faintly redolent of garlic, whip the sour cream slightly, and pile in the centre. Serve with dense rye bread, butter and fresh curd cheese.

Celery and Nut Salad (September)

2 cups sliced heart of celery	¼ cup chopped walnuts
1 cup thinly sliced red peppers	½ cup chopped almonds
1 cup diced apple	lettuce
1 cup grated raw carrot	sour cream dressing

Mix all the ingredients, except lettuce and grated carrot, with the sour cream dressing and put in a lettuce lined bowl. At the last moment, put the grated carrot around the edge and serve without delay.

Egg and Beet Salad

Put sliced boiled beets in lemon juice, sprinkle a little brown sugar over, stir, let stand ½ hour. Liberally dress diced hard-boiled eggs and diced Spanish onion with olive oil, and put in the centre of the dish. Border with the marinaded beets.

Cress, Orange and Banana Salad

Carefully free 2 peeled oranges from membrane and pith, and cut into dice. Mix with 3 sliced bananas and toss in oil and lemon dressing. Sprinkle shredded mint over. Garnish with sprigs of watercress.

Danish Cheese Salad

Dice Danish blue cheese, mix with diced tomato and finely chopped onion (preferably Spanish). Stir in a little sour cream. Pile the mixture on trimmed slices of rye bread. Arrange on a dish, garnish with watercress and olives.

French Bean Salad

Mix cooked, young French beans with diced tomato, a little chopped shallot, and oil and lemon dressing. Garnish with sliced hard-boiled egg.

Raw Vegetable Salad

1 small carrot	½ cup chopped chives
2 artichokes	grated cheese
3 oz. swede	parsley
3 oz. beet	French dressing

Grate the carrot to a juicy mush. Grate the beet and swede. Put each in a separate small dish. Border the beet with minced parsley. Cut the prepared Jerusalem artichokes into very small dice, mix with the chopped chives, toss in French Dressing and put in a separate dish. Arrange the filled dishes on a tray and add a bowl of grated cheese. Serve with home made wholemeal bread and pats of butter.

Tomato Paniers

Cut a slice from the top of each of 6 even-sized tomatoes, remove a little of the pulp so as to leave thick-walled cases. Make 4 downward cuts to within ½ inch of the base of each tomato. Fill each tomato case with Fruit and Vegetable Salad (see p. 92) diced very small and bound with thick mayonnaise; fill to overflowing, so that the tomato 'petals' are separated. Dish up on crisp green lettuce, garnish with olives.

Macaroni and Mushroom Salad

2 cups cooked macaroni
¼ lb. cold, freshly cooked
    mushrooms
1 cup diced cooked carrots

1 tablespoon minced shallot
1 tablespoon minced parsley
pinch of salt
oil and lemon dressing

Rub the salad bowl with a cut clove of garlic, put in the ingredients, add dressing, toss well.

Cream Cheese and Tomato Salad

Blend 4 oz. cream cheese or fresh curd cheese with 2 tablespoons mayonnaise dressing. Halve 6 tomatoes, remove a little of the pulp to form cups, fill generously with the prepared cheese, top with a pinch of minced chervil and tarragon. Put in a border of watercress.

SALAD DRESSINGS

Lemon Milk Dressing

¼ pint unsweetened evaporated milk   juice of 1 lemon

Add the lemon juice to the evaporated milk, stand 1 minute, stir gently till thickened to the consistency of thick cream. As some tinned milks are more concentrated than others, and the acidity of lemons varies, slight modification of the quantities may be needed. The principle remains the same: stir lemon juice into unsweetened evaporated milk.

French Dressing

4 tablespoons olive oil
1 tablespoon lemon juice
pinch each: pepper and sugar

½ teaspoon each: salt and mustard

Mix pepper, sugar, salt and mustard with a little oil to a smooth paste, stir in the rest of the oil, gradually stir in the lemon juice and mix well. To vary, replace half the lemon juice by tarragon vinegar. Official French dressing contains vinegar rather than lemon juice.

Smetana Dressing

½ pint sour cream
1 tablespoon lemon juice

1 tablespoon liquid honey
pinch each: salt and nutmeg

Mix honey and seasonings, stir in the sour cream, whisk till thickened, then gradually stir in the lemon juice.

Fruit Juice Dressing

¼ pint olive oil
2 tablespoons lemon juice
2 tablespoons grapefruit juice

2 tablespoons orange juice
1 tablespoon honey

Mix the ingredients well together with a rotary egg whisk.

Oil and Lemon Dressing

6 tablespoons olive oil	$\frac{1}{4}$ teaspoon salt
1 tablespoon lemon juice	pinch each: pepper and sugar

Blend the salt, sugar and pepper with a few drops of oil. Gradually stir in the rest of the oil and the lemon juice alternately. Mix briskly. The Dressing may be varied as follows:

1. Add $\frac{1}{2}$ teaspoon celery salt with the seasonings.
2. Add finely minced parsley and onion to the dressing.
3. Add 1 teaspoon of chopped capers to the dressing.
4. Add 1 teaspoon of tarragon vinegar to the dressing.
5. Add 1 tablespoon finely chopped olives to the dressing.
6. Add 1 tablespoon of grapefruit juice or orange juice to the dressing.

Lemon Cream Dressing

6 tablespoons lemon juice	$\frac{1}{2}$ teaspoon mustard
3 tablespoons cream	pinch each: salt and pepper
1 teaspoon sugar	

Mix the dry ingredients with a little lemon juice, gradually stir in the rest of the lemon juice, whip the cream and fold in.

Salad Cream (Cooked)

1 teaspoon salt	$\frac{1}{2}$ pint milk
$\frac{3}{4}$ teaspoon mustard (dry)	1 egg
1 teaspoon sugar	3 tablespoons lemon juice
pinch of pepper	1 oz. butter

Mix the dry ingredients in the first column, gradually stir in the beaten egg, stir in the milk. Cook over hot water, stirring constantly, until the sauce thickens. Remove from the heat, stir in the butter a small piece at a time. Stir in the lemon juice.

Curd Cheese Dressing

3 oz. curd cheese	1 tablespoon lemon juice
1 tablespoon mayonnaise	1 tablespoon orange juice
3 tablespoons cream	

Cream the cheese with a fork, stir in the cream and whip until light. Stir in mayonnaise, orange and lemon juice. Good with many salads including fruit salads, for which a pinch of grated orange rind may be stirred into the dressing.

Egg Yolk Dressing (1)

1 yolk of hard-boiled egg	1 teaspoon olive oil
½ teaspoon each: salt, sugar and mustard	juice of ½ lemon
	¼ pint evaporated milk or cream

Add the oil to the dry ingredients and work into a smooth paste. Mix in the yolk of the hard-boiled egg. Gradually stir in the lemon juice, add the cream or unsweetened evaporated milk, stirring constantly.

Egg Yolk Dressing (2)

1 yolk of hard-boiled egg	pinch of pepper
1 raw yolk of egg	¼ pint olive oil
1 teaspoon made mustard	juice of ½ lemon
½ teaspoon salt	

Mash the hard-boiled yolk with the mustard, salt and pepper to a very smooth paste. Gradually stir in a third of the oil. Stir in the beaten raw yolk, then, by degrees, the rest of the oil. Gradually stir in the lemon juice.

Mayonnaise Dressing

(see p. 25 in ' Sauces and Gravies ' Section)

HORS D'ŒUVRE

Celeriac Hors D'Œuvre

Peel the celeriac roots and free them from fibre, cut into ½-inch slices, cover with cold water, simmer 45 minutes, drain. Cut the cooked celeriac into discs with a pastry cutter. Sprinkle with lemon juice, dress with mayonnaise, garnish with hard-boiled egg diced or sliced.

Salsify Hors D'Œuvre

Scrape the roots, drop them into cold water containing a little lemon juice. Cut into 3-inch lengths and boil till tender (about 45 minutes). Drain, cool, dress first with French Dressing then with Smetana dressing. Garnish with olives and parsley.

Cauliflower Hors D'Œuvre

Dress neat sprigs of the curd of cooked cauliflower with Lemon Cream Dressing (see p. 98), dabbed with mayonnaise. Garnish with tiny balls of curd cheese blended with a little Mayonnaise or any sharp Salad Cream.

Vegetable Mayonnaise in Tomatoes

Cut tomatoes sconewise, half way down from the stem end, and remove a little of the pulp. Spread the 'petals' somewhat, and fill the tomatoes with asparagus tips bound with mayonnaise, or with cooked garden peas mixed with finely chopped hard-boiled egg and mayonnaise, or with finely chopped fruit and vegetable salad dressed with thick salad cream.

Portugese Onions Hors D'Œuvre

Put 1 lb. button onions in a casserole with 1 oz. butter, 1 tablespoon hot water, and 2 bay leaves. Cook very gently 3 hours. When quite cold, dish up and coat, first with any salad cream, then with bottled tomato sauce.

Hors D'Œuvre Tray

Place a variety of single items, each in a small dish, on a suitable tray. The following are popular:

1. Small dice of cooked beet in lemon juice.
2. Black, green and stuffed olives, washed and lightly dried.
3. Quartered hard-boiled eggs on a layer of thick sour cream.
4. Asparagus tips in French Dressing.
5. Bottled champignons in olive oil and lemon juice.
6. Thinly sliced black radish with oil and lemon.
7. Sliced tomatoes in Mayonnaise sprinkled with shredded mint.
8. Braised celery, chilled, cut even, spread with Curd Cheese Dressing.
9. Diced fresh cucumber in sour cream.
10. Artichoke bottoms in Mayonnaise.
11. Stuffed tomatoes with a filling of hard-boiled egg, chopped sauerkraut, and tomato pulp bound with Mayonnaise.
12. Aubergine Mayonnaise. Bake an aubergine 45 minutes, cool, peel, mash very smooth with Mayonnaise, nutmeg and pepper. Mask top with Mayonnaise and serve cold.
13. Avocado. Peel the avocado, cut into neat slices $\frac{1}{4}$ inch thick, dress with olive oil.
14. Diced melon in Smetana Dressing.

Pineapple and Grapefruit

Neatly cut small dice of fresh pineapple mixed with sugar cube size dice of grapefruit, sprinkled with lemon juice, dressed with sour cream, garnished with diced tomato.

See also p. 73.

EGG COOKERY

Boiled Eggs and Coddled Eggs

For medium boiled eggs, put the eggs into gently boiling water and cook 3½ minutes. For coddled eggs, put the eggs into fast boiling water but withdraw the heat immediately. Let the eggs stay in the water for 15 minutes. The pan must be kept in a warm place so that the water does not grow cold. Eggs done this way have a creaminess absent from the ordinary boiled egg.

Poached Eggs

Break the eggs gently into a saucer, cup or small bowl, and slip gently into a shallow pan of boiling water. Cook gently until the eggs are just set. Lift with a slice, drain carefully, and serve on hot buttered toast, mashed potatoes, curried vegetables, spinach purée, toasted muffins, or grainily cooked rice flavoured with tomato purée. Various special poachers may be had, and these keep the eggs a neater shape. But the eggs cooked in them are often steamed rather than poached.

Scrambled Eggs

3 eggs   3 tablespoons milk
1 level tablespoon butter   pinch each: salt and pepper

Melt the butter in a small pan. Beat the eggs slightly, add milk and seasoning and mix well. Pour into the pan and cook over very gentle heat, or over hot water, stirring constantly to free the cooked eggs from the pan. Serve hot, as soon as the eggs are lightly set. Tiny pellets of extra butter may be stirred in just when they are done, but not before. In the same way, a little grated cheese, or tomato purée, or chopped casseroled onion or mushroom may be stirred in before serving. It is sometimes said that milk or other liquid should not be added to eggs for scrambling. But the addition undoubtedly makes the eggs more succulent as they must be cooked slowly. The addition of extra butter or a spoonful of cream when the eggs are done is adopted when the milk is omitted. (1-2 portions.)

Eggs sur le Plat

Melt a tablespoon of butter in a shallow fireproof dish, carefully break in two eggs, cook over gentle heat until the eggs are just set. Serve hot, in the dish. The tops of the eggs will not be so thoroughly cooked as the lower surface, but this is the attraction of the dish, provided that the eggs are very fresh and of good quality. Crusty wholemeal rolls, freshly made toast, or dark rye bread and butter are equally good with the dish. (1 portion.)

Eggs in the Glass

An American and German favourite for which soft boiled eggs, or slightly more than soft boiled eggs, are emptied into a tumbler or small buttered glass dish, and served without more ado. Seasoning is added at the table. Rye bread and butter are the usual accompaniments.

French Omelet (2 eggs)

Melt a walnut of butter in a small, clean, but not newly washed omelet pan, and let it melt slowly. Beat the eggs with a pinch of salt and 3 drops of water, make the butter hot but not smoking, and pour in the eggs. At once, lift the edges of the omelet with the tip of a knife so that the fluid egg may flow under. Without waiting, lightly fold the omelet, without regard to particular shape, and while the top is still quite moist. Slip it on to a hot plate and serve at once. (1 portion.) *Note.* For a larger omelet, use 3 or 4 eggs, more butter in proportion, and a somewhat larger pan.

Filled Omelets

Have ready, warming in a small saucepan, 2 or 3 tablespoons of the preferred filling. Proceed as for French Omelet, and put the filling on the omelet just before folding. Popular fillings include: creamed mushrooms, curd of freshly cooked cauliflower blended with cream and a little grated cheese, cream cheese sharpened with a grate of raw onion (this need not be very warm), fried onions and tomatoes, cooked asparagus tips in cream, little peas with freshly shredded mint, diced cooked potato with tomato purée, spinach noodles flavoured with cheese and garlic, Parmesan cheese moistened with cream,

Soufflé Omelet (2 eggs)

Separate the yolks from the whites of the eggs. Whip the whites to a stiff froth. Beat the yolks with a pinch of seasoning and half a teaspoon of water, fold in the whites, pour into the omelet pan containing a dessertspoon of hot melted butter, reduce heat, and cook slowly for 3 minutes. Fold, cook for a minute more, then serve at once on a hot plate. (1 portion.)

Spanish Omelet

Various forms of this are prepared in Spain. *1.* The 'filling' is blended with the beaten eggs, poured into the pan containing hot melted butter, and cooked not quite so quickly as a plain omelet. The omelet is not folded but served flat on a hot dish. *2.* The eggs are slightly stirred during the cooking, the cooking is somewhat less rapid, and the omelet takes no definite shape. The eggs for this are flavoured with a pinch of finely minced garlic. *3.* Two pans are used for this. A simple French Omelet is prepared in each. The filling is quickly put on the surface of one omelet as soon as it begins to set, and the second omelet is neatly placed, moist side down, over the filling. It is cooked for a few more seconds and served on a hot dish.

About Soufflés

The Soufflé, though light and fluffy if correctly made, is packed with concentrated nourishment, for many eggs go to its preparation. It has a plastic basis, the Panada, an extra thick White Sauce made of flour, milk and butter. A distinctive flavouring ingredient is added, such as cheese, spinach, chocolate, ground almonds and so on. The yolks of several eggs blend and bind the ingredients and impart great delicacy. The whites of the eggs are whipped full of air before they are folded in, and cooking heat expands the air so that the Soufflé rises and becomes very light. But when it leaves the oven, the cooler air exerts the opposite effect, and the Soufflé begins to collapse. It should, therefore, be served as soon as it is done. (See Panada recipe, p. 22.)

See Parmesan Soufflé recipe (p. 46) in the Cheese section of Main Course Dishes, also recipe for Mushroom Soufflé (p. 66) in the Egg section of Main Course Dishes. Also, Vermicelli Cheese Soufflé (p. 58) and Coffee Chocolate Soufflé (p. 115).

SWEET DISHES

Baked Sponge Pudding

2 oz. butter	5 oz. self-raising flour
3 oz. sugar	2 tablespoons milk
2 eggs	pinch of salt

Cream butter and sugar, slightly beat the eggs and beat in gradually. Fold in the sifted flour and salt in 3 or 4 lots, adding driblets of the milk in between. Turn the batter into a greased pie dish and bake in a moderate oven, Gas Mark 4, or 350 deg., for 45 to 50 minutes. To vary, add a little grated lemon rind to the batter.

Eve's Pudding

2 cups stewed apples	1 egg
1 oz. butter	2 oz. self-raising flour
1½ oz. sugar	a little milk

Cream the butter and sugar, stir in beaten egg, stir in flour alternating with driblets of milk to form a batter of dropping consistency. Put the apples in a buttered baking dish, spread the batter over, bake in a moderately hot oven, Gas Mark 5, or 375 deg., for 35 minutes. Serve hot with custard sauce. To vary, use other fruits in place of apples.

Gala Pudding

8 thin slices of sponge cake	2 oz. sultanas
1 pint very thick custard	jam for spreading
¼ pint milk	sugar for sprinkling
2 oz. glacé cherries	

Line a well-buttered pie dish with half the cake slices and spread with jam. Stir the fruits into the custard and spread over the jam. Cover with remaining cake slices. Pour in milk. Bake in a slow to moderate oven, Gas Mark 4, or 350 deg., for 1 hour. Serve hot or cold.

French Custard Creams

½ pint milk
2 oz. sugar
1 egg

1 oz. custard powder
⅓ oz. butter
2 drops vanilla

Beat egg, gradually add to the custard powder and slacken with the warmed milk. Add sugar to the rest of the milk, bring to the boil, pour gradually on to the egg mixture while stirring constantly. Stir well over hot water (double pan) for 4 minutes. Off the heat, stir in the butter a pellet at a time, then add vanilla. Pour into small pots and serve cold. *Note.* For Lemon Crême, stir a tablespoon of lemon juice into the mixture towards the end and omit vanilla.

Jam and Cream Tart

short crust pastry (see p. 137)   made cream
apricot jam and strawberry jam

Line a tart plate with thinly rolled pastry dough, put in alternating bands of the two jams, bake till the pastry is done. When cool, pipe Made Cream through a star tube along the lines dividing the jams. To vary, introduce bands of stewed apple, mixed currants and sultanas, bottled cherries, etc. For Made Cornish Cream, see recipe below (p. 112).

Glacé Cherry Pudding

8 oz. self-raising flour
3 oz. margarine
3 oz. soft brown sugar
2 eggs

⅜ pint milk
2 oz. glacé cherries
1 oz. sultanas
pinch of salt

Wash the fruits, dry and roll in flour. Cream the margarine and sugar, stir in the beaten eggs, sift in the blended flour and salt, alternating with driblets of milk. Mix in the fruits. Put the mixture in a buttered pudding basin, cover with greased paper, steam 2 hours. Serve with cherry syrup.

Lemon Meringue Pie

1 oz. plain flour
1 oz. cornflour
1 large lemon
2 eggs
1 pint water
3 oz. caster sugar

whites of 2 eggs
1 oz. sugar for meringue
½ oz. butter
1 prebaked pastry flan case (see
  p. 136 under ' Cakes, Pastries
  and Biscuits ').

Mix flour and cornflour with a little of the water to a smooth paste. Boil the rest of the water with the thinly pared lemon rind for 3 minutes then strain into flour paste, stirring constantly. Stir in the lemon juice. Cook over boiling water, stirring all the time, for 5 minutes or till the mixture thickens. Beat the eggs with the 3 oz. sugar until thick and smooth. Gradually stir the lemon sauce into the sugar-egg mixture. Cook over hot water, stirring, 10 minutes. Remove from heat and beat in the butter a pellet at a time. Then pour mixture into the pastry case. Whip egg whites to froth, gradually dredge in 1 oz. sugar and whip to a firm meringue. Pipe or pile on to pie. Bake in a cool oven, Gas Mark 2, or 300 deg., to tint meringue very slightly. The tinting is sometimes done under the griller. Serve cold. *Note.* Egg yolks may be used for the filling instead of whole eggs.

Pear Crescents

6 oz. self-raising flour	milk to mix
2 oz. margarine	ripe pears
1 oz sugar	jam
pinch of salt	

Sift flour and salt, rub in the margarine, add sugar, mix to clear dough with milk. Roll out very thin, cut into squares about 4 by 4 inches. Put a tiny dab of jam in the centre of each, add a section of soft, ripe pear, roll up very loosely from corner to corner and bring the ends together horseshoe fashion. Put the filled crescents on a well greased baking sheet, brush with milk, bake in a moderately hot oven, Gas Mark 5, or 375 deg., for ½ hour. Good hot or cold.

Queen of Puddings

4 oz. cake crumbs	1 oz. butter
2 eggs	grated rind of ½ a lemon
1 pint milk	2 oz. sugar
1 oz. sugar for meringue	jam

Boil the milk, pour on to the cake crumbs, cook gently for 2 minutes. Cool slightly, stir in butter, sugar, egg yolks and lemon rind. Pour into a buttered dish. Bake 30 minutes in a moderate oven. Spread jam over, cover with meringue made of the whipped egg whites and 1 oz. sugar. Bake 3 minutes in a cool oven to set meringue.

Plum Pudding (Plain)

½ lb. self-raising flour	1 egg
3 oz. shredded nut fat	1 tablespoon black treacle
2 oz. raisins	2 oz. brown sugar
3 oz. currants	milk to mix

Beat the egg with a little milk, stir in to the shredded nut fat, stir in the treacle and sugar, stir in flour and driblets of milk alternately until a light dough is formed. Stir in the fruits and mix well. Turn the mixture into a buttered pudding basin, cover with greased paper, steam 2 hours.

Trifle (Chocolate Iced)

Split a sponge cake into 3 layers. Sandwich 2 layers with strawberry jam and place in the trifle dish. Put a good layer of sliced peaches or other fruit on top, cover with the remaining sponge cake. Pour in a cup of the fruit syrup. Spread Made Cream thickly on top, then chill 10 minutes to set. Ice top with chocolate icing. Serve cold. (See recipe for Made Cornish Cream, p. 112.)

Note. For quickly made chocolate icing, make a smooth cream of 3 oz. icing sugar and a little cold water, then stir in 1 level dessert-spoon dry cocoa powder till well-blended. To vary, work in 1 teaspoon creamed butter.

Rice Custard Pudding

½ lb. rice	1 oz. sugar
1 egg	1 oz. butter
1 pint milk	2 oz. sultanas

Boil the rice tender, drain, stir in the sugar butter and sultanas. Beat egg with milk and pour in. Turn the mixture into a buttered pie dish, bake in a slow oven 1½ to 2 hours. *Note.* For Plain Rice Pudding, do not boil the rice, but bake it as slow as possible, with milk, butter, sugar and grated nutmeg on top.

Sponge Pudding (Steamed)

4 oz. sugar	pinch of salt
2 oz. butter	3 tablespoons milk
2 eggs	jam
6 oz. self-raising flour	

Cream the butter and sugar very light. Beat in the eggs singly. Stir in the sifted flour and salt in three lots with a tablespoon of milk after each. Put 2 tablespoons of jam in the bottom of a buttered pudding mould, turn in the batter, cover with greased paper, steam 2 hours. Serve with jam sauce.

Apple Meringue Flan

stewed apples (1 lb. uncooked)
1 cup setting custard
jam for spreading

1 prebaked flan case
meringue of white of 1 egg and
1 oz. sugar

Spread a film of jam in the flan case. Add the drained stewed apples, cover with thick custard. Whip the white of the egg to a froth, gradually beat in the sugar to form a firm meringue. Spread meringue over custard. Place in a cool oven, Gas Mark 2, or 300 deg., for 5 minutes or until top is delicately tinted; or tint lightly under the griller. Serve hot or cold. *Note 1.* Other sweet fruits may replace apples. *2.* For Flan Case, see recipe in Cakes, Pastries and Biscuits section (p. 136).

Apple and Walnut Slices

6 oz. self-raising flour
2½ oz. butter or margarine
stewed apples (2 lb. uncooked)
1 cup custard thickening
pinch of salt

1 oz. shelled walnuts
½ teaspoon grated lemon rind
milk to mix
sugar to sprinkle

Mix flour and salt, rub in butter or margarine, stir in sugar and lemon rind, mix to a smooth dough with cold milk. Roll out and line a greased oblong baking tin, reserving some dough for latticing. Dust pastry with flour. Mix custard thickening with drained stewed apples and walnuts chopped fine, spread evenly over the pastry. Roll reserved dough thin, cut into ½-inch wide strips, and fix to dampened edges of the pastry. Bake in a moderate oven, Gas Mark 5, or 375 deg., for 35 minutes or until pastry browns. When cold cut into slices. *Note.* To prepare Custard Thickening, moisten a tablespoon of custard powder with a little cold water to a smooth paste. Sweeten a cup of stewed fruit liquid, boil, then pour on to the paste, stirring. Stir and cook over gentle heat 1 minute.

Apple Dumplings (Baked)

5 or 6 apples   butter
about ½ lb. short crust pastry   cinnamon
brown sugar

Roll out the pastry into 5 or 6 thin rounds large enough to contain apples, and make 4 or 5 inch cuts around the edges. Place a pared and cored apple in the centre of each, fill cavities with sugar, butter and cinnamon. Wet edges of pastry, gather up, and press gently at top to seal. Turn top side down on a greased tin, bake in a pastry oven till the pastry is done, wash tops with a little warm water, sprinkle sugar over, and put back in the oven for 2 minutes. Serve hot.

Apple Strudel

For the pastry:

½ lb. self-raising flour   grated rind of ½ lemon
yolks of 2 eggs   milk to mix
3 oz. butter   pinch of salt
2 oz. caster sugar

For the filling:

2 lb. drained stewed apples   butter for dotting
½ lb. soaked seedless raisins   1 cup custard thickening (see
2 oz. currants   recipe, Apple and Walnut
cinnamon for sprinkling   Slices)

Sift flour and salt together, stir in the sugar, rub in the butter. Make a hollow, put in the lemon rind, egg yolks beaten with a little milk and sufficient milk to make a dough that will roll easily. Divide the dough into 3 pieces and roll each into a very thin sheet to fit a Yorkshire pudding tin. Line the well-greased tin with one of the pastry sheets. Mix apples, raisins, currants and custard thickening, and spread half the mixture over the pastry lining. Dot with butter and sprinkle well with cinnamon. Cover with another sheet of the pastry, repeat the fruit filling, top with the last pastry sheet, brush with milk. Bake in a moderately hot oven, Gas Mark 5, or 375 deg., about 40 minutes or till the pastry is well done. When cold, cut into neat squares and sprinkle liberally with sugar. *Note.* An ounce of chopped nuts may be added to the fruit filling for variation.

Bakewell Pudding

1 egg	1 oz. ground almonds
2 oz. butter	1 tablespoon milk
2 oz. caster sugar	short crust pastry
jam for spreading	1 oz. sugar for meringue
1 oz. self-raising flour	

Line a Victoria sandwich tin or similar container with thinly rolled pastry, and spread with a film of jam. Cream butter and sugar, beat in the yolk of the egg, fold in the flour, stir in ground almonds. Spread mixture over jam. Bake in a fairly hot oven, Gas Mark 6, or 400 deg., for ½ hour. Beat white of egg to a snow, gradually beat in 1 oz. sugar, pile roughly over the baked pudding. Place in a cool oven for 2 minutes or so, to tinge meringue.

Baked Jam Roll

½ lb. self-raising flour	½ lb. raspberry or strawberry jam
3 oz. margarine	milk to mix
pinch of salt	

Sift flour and salt together, rub in margarine, mix to a soft dough with milk. Roll out into an oblong about ½ inch thick, spread jam over to within an inch of the edges, moisten edges, roll up very loosely. Bake on a greased tin in a hot oven, Gas Mark 7, or 425 deg. Serve hot with jam sauce.

Vermicelli Raisin Pudding

4 oz. vermicelli	1 dessertspoon golden syrup
2 eggs	1 tablespoon sugar
1 oz. butter	½ pint milk
2 oz. seedless raisins	pinch each: salt and nutmeg

Boil the vermicelli in 1 pint water 7 minutes. Drain, cool, stir in the butter, raisins, syrup, sugar, seasonings, and lastly, the eggs beaten up in the milk. Pour into a buttered casserole and bake 2 hours in a slow oven, Gas Mark 2, or 300 deg. To vary, add 1 oz. halved glacé cherries to the mixture before baking.

Madeira Pudding

2 eggs
3 oz. butter
4 oz. sugar
4 oz. self-raising flour

2 oz. sultanas
1 oz. candied peel
grated rind of ½ lemon
pinch of salt

Cream butter and sugar, stir in beaten eggs alternating with the blended flour and salt. Beat well. Add sultanas, cut peel and lemon rind. Turn into a well-buttered mould, cover with greased paper, steam 1¾ hours.

Made Cornish Cream

1 oz. fresh butter (unsalted) or margarine (vegetarian)
1 tea cup milk

1 level dessertspoon custard powder
½ level teaspoon sugar

Moisten the custard powder with a little of the cold milk and mix to a smooth paste. Boil the rest of the milk, pour on to paste while stirring. Cook and stir over hot water for 2 minutes. Let cool till lukewarm. Meanwhile, add sugar to butter and cream very light indeed. Now combine, gradually, the lukewarm blanc mange with the creamed butter, whipping constantly. A rich, thick cream results, and one that is good to pile on fruit tarts, trifles, light cakes and pastries. It is equally good with cold puddings, stewed fruits, and as a filling for sponge sandwiches, light yeast buns (Devon Splits), and scones. *Note.* A tiny pinch of New Zealand agar whipped into the cream at the last, stabilizes it, and keeps it firm in cake fillings, etc. A ½ oz. extra butter makes an extra-rich cream. It keeps for 12 hours, or longer in cold weather.

Manchester Pudding

4 oz. cake crumbs
1 pint milk
2 eggs
1 oz. sugar for meringue

2 oz. sugar for filling
grated rind of ½ lemon
short crust pastry
jam

Boil milk and pour over mixed crumbs and sugar. Cool, then stir in the beaten yolks of the eggs and the lemon rind. Line the edges only of a greased pie dish with thinly rolled pastry. Put a layer of jam in the bottom of the dish, pour in the egg and crumb mixture, bake 45 minutes in a moderately hot oven, Gas Mark 5, or 375 deg. Whip whites of eggs to stiff snow, beat in the sugar, when firm, pile on top of the baked pudding and return to a cool oven for 2 or 3 minutes. Serve hot.

Tutti Frutti Noodle Pudding

½ lb. egg noodles or ribbon macaroni
1 egg
1 oz. butter
2 oz. sugar
nutmeg

1 oz. custard powder
2 oz. currants
1 oz. sultanas
1 oz. glacé cherries
½ pint milk
butter for dotting

Boil the noodles quite tender, drain, stir in the butter, a grate of nutmeg and 1 oz. of the sugar. Whip white of the egg stiff and fold in. Make a paste of the custard powder with a little cold milk, boil the rest of the milk with the remaining sugar, pour on to the paste, stir and cook 2 minutes over simmering heat. Remove from heat, cool a little, and stir in the yolk of the egg and the fruits. Put half the noodle mixture in a buttered pie dish, spread the fruit-custard filling over. Dot with butter, stand dish in a tin of boiling water, cover with a greased paper, bake in a moderate oven 1 hour.

Ginger Sultana Pudding

4 oz. fine bread crumbs
2 oz. brown sugar
2 oz. margarine
2 eggs

1 teaspoon ginger
1 teaspoon cinnamon
2 oz. sultanas
¼ pint milk

Scald milk, pour on to bread crumbs while mixing with a wooden spoon. Cream the butter and sugar and stir into the mixture. Stir in the beaten eggs, spices and fruit. Steam the mixture in buttered pudding mould, covered with greased paper, for 1¼ hours. Serve with melted syrup.

Ginger Sponge Pudding

1 oz. butter
1 oz sugar
1 tablespoon treacle
1 egg
5 oz. self-raising flour

1 level teaspoon ginger
1 teaspoon cinnamon
pinch of salt
milk to mix

Cream the butter and sugar, stir in the egg beaten with some milk, the treacle, the blended flour, salt and spices, alternating with driblets of milk to produce a thick pouring batter. Pour into a buttered mould, cover, steam 1¼ hours. Serve with Custard Sauce or syrup.

Gingerbread Pudding

8 oz. self-raising flour	1 tablespoon brown sugar
4 oz. margarine	1 teaspoon ginger
1 egg	1 teaspoon cinnamon
¼ pint milk	pinch salt
¼ pint black treacle	

Sift flour, salt and spices into a bowl. Rub in margarine. Beat the egg and milk together and pour in. Mix in the sugar and treacle. Pour into a greased pie dish and bake about 1 hour in a moderately hot oven, Gas Mark 5, or 375 deg. Serve hot with Custard Sauce or melted treacle.

Curd Cheese Tart (Käsekuchen)

For the pastry:	*For the filling:*
6 oz. self-raising flour	½ lb. curd cheese
1½ oz. butter	1 egg
1 dessertspoon salad oil	2 tablespoons sugar
1½ oz. sugar	1 teaspoon cornflour
4 tablespoons milk	5 tablespoons milk
pinch grated lemon rind	1 oz. sultanas
pinch salt	

Pastry: mix flour, sugar and salt, rub in the butter, make a hollow, pour in the oil and milk, add lemon rind, mix to soft dough. Roll out ⅜ inch thick and line a greased tin 7 by 7 by 1½ inches. Reserve some of the dough for latticing top.
Filling: moisten cornflour with the milk, add to cheese, cream up thoroughly. Gradually stir in the beaten egg. Stir in sugar and sultanas. Turn the filling into the pastry shell. Roll reserve pastry very thin and cut into strips ½ inch wide. Lattice top in squares or diamonds, brush with milk. Bake 35 minutes in a moderate oven, Gas Mark 4, or 350 deg. When cold, cut into neat slices, squares or triangles.

Compote of Fruits

Fruits are carefully prepared and stewed very gently without sugar. They must not become mushy. Small, even-sized apples are suitable. They are thinly pared, cored and stewed whole. The liquid is carefully strained off, sweetened with 1 oz. sugar to each ½ pint and boiled 5 minutes to form syrup. Pour the syrup over the fruit, add any preferred flavouring, chill well before serving. Whipped Cream, Made Cream, Devonshire Cream, or ice cream are the usual accompaniments. Pears, peaches, large prunes, apricots, cherries, are suitable for this dish, either singly or in any preferred combination.

Coffee Chocolate Soufflé

1½ oz. cocoa	1 oz. flour
2 tablespoons strong black coffee	¼ pint milk
2 oz. sugar	4 eggs
1¼ oz. butter	

Mix sugar and cocoa, moisten to a smooth paste with the coffee, boil the milk and pour on to the paste, stirring well. Return to pan, let boil, then keep hot. Melt butter in a saucepan, stir in the flour, cook and stir over gentle heat for 2 minutes: add the cocoa mixture and cook and stir constantly for 3 minutes over gentle heat. Off the heat, beat in the egg yolks singly, then fold in the stiffly whipped whites of the eggs. Turn the mixture into a buttered soufflé mould lined with a high paper band. Bake in a moderate oven, Gas Mark 4, or 350 deg., for 20 minutes. Serve immediately. *Note.* For Soufflés see p. 104.

Cherry Cobbler

2 cups stewed or bottled cherries	2 oz. sugar
1 cup custard thickening	grated rind of ½ lemon
4 oz. self-raising flour	pinch of salt
1 oz. butter	milk to mix

Mix cherries with custard thickening (see recipe, Apple and Walnut Slices, p. 109), and put in a greased pie dish. Sift flour and salt, rub in the butter, add sugar and lemon rind and mix to soft dough with milk. Roll the dough to the size of the dish and spread over fruit. Bake in a hot oven, Gas Mark 7, or 425 deg., for 15 minutes.

Serve warm, with cherry syrup. *Note.* For a richer dish, add the yolk of an egg to the dough. To vary, make Cobbler Pies with other fruits such as pears, bilberries, loganberries, raspberries or mixed fruits.

Chocolate Sponge Pudding

5 oz. self-raising flour	1 tablespoon golden syrup
1 oz. cocoa	2½ oz. margarine
1 egg	3 tablespoons milk
2 oz. sugar	

Sift flour and cocoa. Cream the margarine and sugar, stir in the syrup, stir in beaten egg, stir in flour and milk alternately. Steam in a covered, greased mould for 2 hours. Unmould after standing 3 minutes. Serve hot with Chocolate-Coffee Sauce. (See p. 26.)

Boiled Batter Pudding

2 eggs	pinch of salt
1 pint milk	2 oz. currants
½ lb. self-raising flour	

Sift flour and salt together, make a hollow, put in the eggs beaten with ¼ of the milk, gradually beat in the rest of the milk and whisk to a thick batter. Butter a pudding mould and sprinkle with the cleaned currants. Pour in the batter to within an inch of the rim. Cover with paper. Boil 2 hours. Serve with melted jam. (See also Yorkshire Pudding, p. 156.)

Bread and Butter Pudding

6 slices bread and butter	currants or sultanas
1 pint milk	brown sugar
2 eggs	nutmeg

Sprinkle the bottom of a well-buttered pie dish with fruit, cover with crustless bread and butter, sprinkle sugar and grated nutmeg over. Repeat until the dish is three-quarters full. Beat the eggs and milk, and pour in. Stand 45 minutes. Bake in a moderately hot oven, Gas Mark 5, or 375 deg., for 1 hour. *Note.* The pudding may be steamed instead of baked and served with melted jam.

Blackberry and Apple Pie

3 cups sliced apples (sweetened)   short crust pastry
2 cups ripe blackberries   sugar for sprinkling

Put apples and berries in a saucepan with sugar to taste, and simmer gently till the apples are soft, then turn into a pie dish, juice and all. Grease the edge of the dish, roll out pastry ¼ inch thick, and cover fruit. Bake in a pastry oven till the pastry is done. *Note.* To vary, mix the fruits with ½ cup Custard Thickening (see p. 109) prepared from the fruit juices, and use ½ cup less juice for the pie filling. Sprinkle pie liberally with sugar when taken from the oven. Short crust pastry may be replaced by richer, sweeter pastry.

WHOLEWHEAT BREAD, CAKES AND PUDDINGS

Wholewheat Bread

3 lb. wholewheat flour	1 teaspoon sugar
¾ oz. salt	1 oz. margarine
1 oz. yeast	1 quart warm water

Mix salt with flour. Put yeast and sugar in a cup, pour on a tablespoon warm water, stir till dissolved. Melt the margarine. Make a hollow in the flour, put in the dissolved yeast. Gradually stir in about a third of the warm water, add the melted margarine, then the rest of the warm water, mix well. Knead the dough with the hand 5 minutes. The dough is moist at this stage, but this should not minimize the kneading. Let the dough stand in a warm place, covered with a fresh cloth, for 1 hour.

Knead back the dough, cover, and let stand in the warm place a further ½ hour. Divide the dough into 3 portions, mould each into a round 'bun', flatten with the edge of the hand into an oblong, fold in 3, half turn the dough, fold over once, then put into warm, well greased loaf tins. Let stand, covered lightly so that the cloth does not stick to the rising dough, in the warm place for a further 15 minutes. Bake in a hot oven, Gas Mark 7, or 425 deg., for 1 hour or just under, depending upon the size of the loaves.*

Note 1. Keep the dough warm and free from draughts all through the bread making. *2.* About 1 cup of additional flour should be at hand for dusting the board while cutting and moulding the dough. *3.* Three-quarters of an oz. of salt is 3 heaped teaspoons. *4.* The water must not be hot but warm. *5.* 'Wholemeal' is not necessarily wholewheat, and might be a mixture of various ingredients.

Wholewheat Dinner Rolls

1 lb. wholewheat flour	1 teaspoon sugar
1 heaped teaspoon salt	½ oz. margarine
1 oz. yeast.	¾ pint warm water

* Bread is baked in the uppermost part of the oven, *i.e.* the hottest part.

Mix the dough, and knead it, as directed in the above recipe for wholewheat bread, but add the last of the water cautiously so that the dough does not become too soft. Flours vary in their capacity for holding water. Withhold a little of the water if necessary, but a soft dough is required. Let the dough rise 1 hour, knead back, and let rise 20 minutes, then divide into balls of dough weighing 2 oz. each. Mould into balls, set them on a greased baking sheet, allowing a little space between them, let stand 25 minutes, warm and lightly covered, bake 35 minutes, top shelf, in a hot oven, Gas Mark 6, or 400 deg.

Wholewheat Raisin Cake

½ lb. wholewheat flour	2 oz. caster sugar
1 teaspoon baking powder	2 eggs
4 oz. butter	4 oz. raisins
grated rind of ½ lemon	pinch salt
2 oz. soft brown sugar	milk to mix

Cream the butter, add the sugars and cream again. Add the eggs singly beating them well in. Gradually stir in the blended flour, salt and baking powder, alternating with driblets of milk to keep batter moist but not slack. Stir in the lemon rind and the cleaned flour-dusted fruit. Turn into a paper-lined tin. Bake in a moderately hot oven, Gas Mark 5, or 375 deg., for 1 hour or till done.

Wholewheat Fruit Scones

¾ lb. wholewheat flour	1½ oz. soft brown sugar
2 heaped teaspoons baking powder	3 oz. seedless raisins (or mixed currants and raisins)
1½ oz. butter or margarine	grated rind of ½ lemon
pinch salt	milk to mix

Mix wholewheat flour, salt and baking powder. Rub in the butter or margarine. Make a hollow, put in the sugar, lemon rind, and ½ cup milk, mix to a soft dough, adding milk as required, and mix in the cleaned fruit last. Divide the dough into 3 portions, pat each into a round on a floured board, mark with the back of a knife into scones, but do not cut quite through. Put the scones on a lightly greased and flour-dusted baking sheet, brush with milk, let stand 10 minutes, then bake in a hot oven, Gas Mark 6, or 400 deg. To vary, use 2 tablespoons salad oil instead of butter or margarine, putting this in the hollow with the sugar and milk.

Wholewheat Batter Pudding

6 oz. self-raising wholewheat ¾ pint milk and water
    flour   1 level teaspoon salt
2 eggs   1 oz. margarine

Mix flour and salt, make a hollow, put in the eggs and a little milk,
mix to a smooth paste. Gradually stir in the rest of the liquid and
whisk thoroughly. Make the margarine very hot in a Yorkshire
pudding tin, pour in the batter, bake ½ hour in a hot oven. Cut
into squares and serve hot with gravy.

Wholewheat Rolls (Yeastless)

¾ lb. wholewheat flour   ¾ oz. margarine
¾ oz. baking powder   ½ pint water or milk and water
1 level dessertspoon black   ½ teaspoon salt
    treacle

Mix flour, salt and baking powder in a bowl. Rub in the margarine.
Add the milk and treacle and lightly mix to a dough. Shape into
small rolls, place on lightly greased, flour-dusted tins. Bake in a
hot oven, Gas Mark 7, or 425 deg., for 20 minutes.

Wholewheat Tea Bread

1 lb. wholewheat flour   1 oz. caster sugar
3 oz. butter or margarine   ¾ oz. baking powder
¼ teaspoon salt   about ½ pint milk
1 oz. soft brown sugar

Mix flour, baking powder and salt. Rub in the butter or margarine.
Stir sugar into milk, and add. Mix to dough with milk, using no
more than is necessary to form a soft dough. Roll lightly to a sheet
1 inch thick, and place on a lightly greased and floured baking tin.
bake in a hot oven, Gas Mark 6, or 400 deg. Slice and butter when
cold.
Note. To vary, add any of the following to the dough before
rolling out: *1.* 2 oz. grated cheese. *2.* 2 oz. chopped dates.
3. 1 oz. chopped walnuts. *4.* 2 oz. either raisins or currants, or
chopped figs. *5.* Either the yolk or white of an egg, or 1 oz.
beaten whole egg. Brush top with milk or beaten egg or melted
butter before baking.

Wholewheat Parkin

¾ lb. wholewheat flour
2 oz. coarse oatmeal
4 oz. butter
3 tablespoons black treacle
1 egg

1 teaspoon ginger
1 teaspoon mixed spice
½ teaspoon cinnamon
½ teaspoon bicarbonate of soda
½ pint milk

Put flour, oatmeal and spices in a bowl. Slowly melt butter, stir in the sugar and pour into flour. Stir in treacle, cold milk, beaten egg and the soda dissolved in a little milk. Mix thoroughly and pour batter into a paper-lined tin keeping the batter 1 inch deep. Bake in a slow oven, Gas Mark 1, or 290 deg., for 1½ hours.

Wholewheat Fruit Slices

6 oz. wholewheat flour
2 oz. soft brown sugar
grated rind of ½ lemon
1 teaspoon cinnamon

3 oz. margarine
1 pint stewed apples
4 oz. currants
milk to mix

Rub the margarine into the flour. Add the sugar and lemon rind and sufficient milk to mix to a smooth dough. Divide and roll into 2 very thin sheets. Put one in a shallow greased tin, dust with flour, then spread with the drained stewed apples mixed with the currants. Sprinkle cinnamon over and extra sugar if liked. Cover with the remaining pastry sheet, brush with milk, bake in a moderately hot oven, Gas Mark 5, or 375 deg., for ½ hour. When cold cut into slices or squares.

Wholewheat and Oatmeal Biscuits

½ lb. wholewheat flour
2 oz. fine oatmeal
pinch salt
3 tablespoons olive oil

3 oz. soft brown sugar
1 egg
milk to mix

Mix flour, salt and oatmeal in a bowl, make a hollow, put in the beaten egg, oil and sugar. Mix to a firm dough, adding only sufficient milk to mix. Roll out thinly on a floured board. Cut with a pastry cutter into rounds, place on greased tins, brush with milk, dock with the prongs of a fork, bake in a moderately hot oven, Gas Mark 5, or 375 deg., about 20 minutes or till light brown.

Wholewheat Ginger Pudding

5 oz. wholewheat flour
1 egg
1½ oz. butter
1 tablespoon treacle
1 tablespoon soft brown sugar

½ teaspoon ginger
½ teaspoon mixed spice
⅛ teaspoon bicarbonate of soda
pinch salt

Mix flour, salt, soda and spices, rub in the butter, add the treacle and beaten egg but no other liquid. Mix thoroughly, pour into a greased pudding basin so that it is three-quarters full, cover with a greased paper, steam 1¼ hours. Serve with melted treacle and custard sauce.

Wholemeal Fig Pudding

4 oz. wholemeal bread crumbs
4 oz. wholewheat flour
1 teaspoon baking powder
4 oz. soft brown sugar
2 eggs
4 oz. margarine

4 oz. chopped figs
1 oz. ground almonds
½ teaspoon cinnamon
3 thin slices lemon
pinch salt
¼ pint milk

Grate the margarine and rub into the blended flour, salt, spice and baking powder. Stir in the bread crumbs, almonds, sugar, figs, beaten eggs and milk. Put the lemon slices in the bottom of a buttered pudding mould, put in the batter, cover with greased paper, steam 2 hours. Serve with custard sauce.

Baked Wholewheat Fruit Roly

½ lb. wholewheat flour
3 oz. margarine
1 dessertspoon salad oil
2 oz sugar

grated rind of ½ lemon
6 oz. mixed dried fruit
milk to mix

Mix flour and sugar, rub in the margarine, add lemon rind, mix oil with a little milk and add. Mix to an elastic dough with a little milk. Roll out thinly on a floured table, cover with the cleaned fruits, roll up loosely, bring ends of roll together to form a letter 'U'. Place on a greased tin, brush with milk, bake in a moderately hot oven, Gas Mark 5, or 375 deg., for about 40 minutes. Good hot or cold. *Note.* To vary, the fruits may include a selection of the following: seedless raisins, currants, glacé cherries, sliced dates or figs, dried bananas and soaked prunes. For coconut flavour, add 1 oz. of grated coconut cream (stocked by Health Food Stores).

CAKES, PASTRIES AND BISCUITS

Yorkshire Tea Cakes

2 oz. plain flour   1 oz. fresh yeast
½ pint warm milk (90 deg.)   1 teaspoon sugar

Dissolve yeast and sugar in a tablespoon of warm milk, stir in the rest of the milk gradually, alternating with the flour. Mix till smooth. Cover with a clean, light cloth. Stand in a warm place ½ hour. Then add the following ingredients in the order stated, stirring each one in before adding the next, and adding the flour in 2 or 3 lots.

1 beaten egg   ¼ teaspoon salt
3 oz. sugar   3 oz. warmed margarine
1 lb. plain flour

Knead the dough lightly for 3 or 4 minutes, flouring the hands now and then. Cover the dough and stand in the warm place ½ hour. Now, knead back the dough, cut it into 2-oz. pieces, mould into round 'buns', then roll lightly with a rolling pin into teacakes. Put the cakes on greased tins, dock the centres lightly with a fork, cover and let prove in the warm place for ½ hour. Bake 12 minutes in a moderately hot oven, Gas Mark 5, or 375 deg. For Currant Tea Cakes add 5 oz. well-cleaned currants to the dough after all the flour has been added.

Devon Cream Splits

Prepare the dough as in the Yorkshire Tea Cake recipe, weigh off 1-oz. pieces, mould, prove and bake as directed. When cold, cut a slit in the side of each, insert a blob of whipped cream or made cream, garnish with a spot of red jam, dust icing sugar over.

Iced Tea Rings

Following the recipe for Yorkshire Tea Cakes, weigh off the dough into 4-oz. pieces, roll each piece under the hands into a 12-inch

123

rope. Twist pairs of the ropes together, join ends to form rings. Prove and bake as directed. When almost cool, spread the tops thinly with water icing flavoured with lemon juice. Before the icing sets, sprinkle with flaked almonds.

Curd Cheese Homentash

Prepare the dough as in Yorkshire Tea Cake recipe. Weigh off the dough into 2-oz. pieces, roll out on a floured board into rounds ¼ inch thick. Blend fresh curd cheese with a little sugar and a few sultanas, and put a dessertspoon of the mixture on the centre of each round. Bring 3 sides of each round to overlap at the centre forming triangular cakes. Brush with warm milk, prove and bake as directed. Serve cold.

Dundee Cake

4 oz. butter	½ lb. sultanas
4 oz. sugar	¼ lb. currants
3 eggs	1 oz. glacé cherries
½ lb. self-raising flour	2 oz. cut candied peel
pinch salt	grated rind of 1 lemon
½ teaspoon mixed spice	blanched almonds for top

Cream the butter and sugar together till very light. Add the eggs one at a time, stirring each in thoroughly. Sift flour, spice and salt together and stir in gradually. Mix in the cleaned fruits and lemon rind. Turn the batter into a double paper-lined cake tin. Arrange blanched almonds all over top. Bake about 1½ hours, middle shelf, Gas Mark 4, or 360 deg.

Rich Dundee Cake

½ lb. butter	¼ teaspoon baking powder
4 oz. caster sugar	10 oz. sultanas
4 oz. soft brown sugar	2 oz. currants
5 eggs	2 oz. cut candied peel
2 oz. ground almonds	2 oz. glacé cherries
½ lb. plain flour	grated rind of ½ lemon
pinch salt	blanched almonds for top

Cream the butter, add the sugars and cream again until very light. Beat in the eggs one at a time. Sift in the blended flour, salt and baking powder and stir, very gently at this stage, till smooth. Stir in the ground almonds, cleaned fruits and grated lemon rind. Turn the batter into a cake tin doubly lined with greased paper. Cover top with blanched almonds. Bake about 1½ hours, Gas Mark 4, or 360 deg.

Seed Cake

8 oz. self-raising flour	2 eggs
4 oz. butter	1 tablespoon carraway seeds
4½ oz. sugar	4 tablespoons milk
1 dessertspoon cornflour	pinch salt

Cream the butter, add the sugar and cream again. Add the eggs singly, beating each in thoroughly. Sift the flour and salt together and gradually stir into the batter, alternating with driblets of the milk. Stir in the seeds, reserving a few for the top. Turn the batter into a paper-lined tin, sprinkle seeds over, bake on middle shelf, about 1¼ hours in a moderately hot oven, Gas Mark 5, or 375 deg.

Cherry Cake

½ lb. caster sugar	4 oz. glacé cherries
6 oz. butter or margarine	4 tablespoons milk
3 eggs	grated rind of ½ lemon
1 lb. self-raising flour	6 drops vanilla essence

Cream the butter or margarine, add sugar and cream again till very light. Add the eggs singly and beat well in. Sift in the flour in 5 lots, alternating with driblets of the milk. Stir in the rind and essence. Stir in the washed, dried and flour-dusted cherries, reserving one-third. Turn the batter into paper-lined tins, gently press reserved cherries just below the surface of the cakes. Bake in a moderately hot oven, Gas Mark 5, or 375 deg., for about 1¼ hours or until the cakes are golden brown. *Note.* A little angelica is sometimes added.

Cream Sponge Slices

1¾ oz. butter	½ teaspoon baking powder
3 oz. caster sugar	4 tablespoons milk
1 egg	3 drops lemon or vanilla essence
jam and cream to sandwich	
4½ oz. self raising flour	

Cream butter, add sugar and cream again until very light. Stir in the beaten egg and whisk for 2 or 3 minutes. Sift in the blended flour and baking powder in 4 lots alternating with the milk. Add the essence. The batter must not be beaten after flour has been added. Turn the batter into a paper-lined tin about 7 by 7 by 1 inches. Bake 25 minutes in a moderately hot oven, Gas Mark 5, or 375 deg. When cold, cut into 2 layers, spread lower layer with jam, then with whipped cream or made cream. Gently replace top layer, sprinkling, if liked, with sifted icing sugar. Cut into 12 even slices.

Eclairs

3 eggs	pinch of salt
4 oz. flour	filling cream
2 oz. butter or margarine	icing
⅛ pint water	

Put the butter or margarine, the salt and water in a saucepan. Heat to boiling point then stir in the flour. Reduce heat and stir constantly with a wooden spoon till the paste comes clean away from the bottom and sides of the pan, then remove from the heat. Break open the ball of paste, cool a little, then beat in the eggs one at a time, working the paste constantly till it is light and smooth. Put the paste in a forcing bag with a plain eclair tube and pipe out 3½-inch lengths on to greased tins, leaving space for the eclairs to expand. Bake 20 minutes in a hot oven, Gas Mark 8, or 450 deg. When cold, split the Eclairs with a sharp pointed knife and sandwich with whipped cream or made cream. Ice the tops lightly with white or coffee icing. *Note.* The oven door must not be opened while the Eclairs are baking. Bake just above middle shelf.

Chocolate Gateau

2 oz. butter	4 oz. self-raising flour
3 oz. caster sugar	¾ oz. cocoa powder
2 eggs	2 tablespoons milk

Cream the butter and sugar. Stir in the eggs singly and beat well. Dissolve the cocoa in 2 tablespoons of boiling water added gradually; when the cocoa paste is cool, stir it into the batter. Stir in the sifted flour, alternating with driblets of the milk. Turn the batter into a paper-lined tin—about 7 by 7 by 1 inches. Bake ½ hour in a moderate oven, Gas Mark 4, or 360 deg. The cake when cold may be finished by cutting it into 2 layers, sandwiching with made cream, and icing the top with white or chocolate icing. Or it may be cut into 3 layers and sandwiched with jam between the lower layers, and chocolate butter cream between the upper layers. *Note.* To make the Butter Cream, cream 1 oz. butter with 1 oz. icing sugar and 1 oz. chocolate powder.

Chocolate Cup Cakes

2 oz. butter
2½ oz. caster sugar
1 large egg
4 oz. self-raising flour

½ oz. cocoa powder
pinch bicarbonate of soda
3 tablespoons milk

Cream the butter, add the sugar and cream again. Stir in the beaten egg and blend thoroughly. Sift in the blended flour and cocoa, alternating with driblets of milk in which the soda is dissolved. Turn the batter into little paper baking cases (about 16) filling them two-thirds full. Put the cups on a tin and bake 18 minutes in a moderate oven, Gas Mark 4, or 360 deg. When the cakes are cold the tops may be chocolate iced.

Chocolate Whirls

3 oz. butter
3 oz. caster sugar
½ beaten egg
6 oz. self-raising flour

½ oz. cocoa powder
pinch of cinnamon
milk to mix

Cream the butter and sugar, add the beaten egg, stir smooth. Mix cocoa and cinnamon with a quarter of the flour and stir into the batter. Gradually stir in the rest of the flour moistening the batter from time to time with driblets of milk. The batter, however, must be kept firm. Put the batter in a forcing bag with a large star tube and pipe whirls on to a lightly greased, flour-dusted tin. Stand 2 hours in a cool place. Place tin on another tin to protect bottoms from scorching. Bake in a moderate oven, Gas Mark 4, or 360 deg., for 20 minutes or until the whirls are done.

Petits Fours

11 oz. flour
1 oz. cornflour
½ teaspoon baking powder
pinch of salt

4 eggs
½ lb. butter
½ lb. sugar
4 drops vanilla essence

Cream the butter and sugar very light. Beat in the eggs singly. Stir in the sifted flours, baking powder, and salt. Add the essence of vanilla last. Spread the batter ¾ inch deep in a greased tin. Bake in a moderate oven, Gas Mark 4, or 360 deg., for about 25 minutes or till the cake is lightly tinted. When cold, split with a sharp knife into 2 layers, sandwich with butter icing, or jam, or butter cream blended with ground almonds. Ice top and cut into small neat bars, lozenges, squares, etc. *Note*. For Butter Icing, work dry icing sugar into butter till thick and smooth.

Paris Almond Petits Fours

½ lb. caster sugar   whites of 3 eggs
½ lb. ground almonds   6 drops almond essence

Mix the ground almonds and sugar. Moisten with the egg whites and beat well. Stand the pan in a bowl of hot water and continue to stir until the paste is slightly warm. Put it in a forcing bag with a star tube, and pipe various small shapes on to flour-dusted, lightly greased tins. Let stand 12 hours. Bake for a few minutes in a sharp oven, Gas Mark 6, or 400 deg., until the points of the biscuits are browned.

Butter Biscuits

1 lb. self-raising flour   2 eggs
½ lb. butter   ½ cup milk
½ lb. sugar   4 oz. sultanas

Cream butter and sugar. Stir in the eggs singly. Stir in the sifted flour, and milk. Add the sultanas last. Work into a firm dough adding a little more flour if necessary. Roll out ¼ inch thick on a floured board. Cut with 2-inch pastry cutter into rounds. Bake in a moderate oven, Gas Mark 4, or 360 deg., for 10 to 12 minutes or until crisp.

Almond Shortbreads

½ lb. plain flour   1 oz. ground almonds
¼ teaspoon baking powder   2 eggs
4 oz. butter   4 drops almond essence
4 oz. caster sugar

Sift flour and baking powder into a bowl, rub in the butter with the finger tips until the mixture resembles fine bread crumbs. Make a hollow, put in the sugar, ground almonds, essence and the beaten eggs. Mix to an elastic dough, adding a little more flour if necessary. Roll out rather less than ½ inch thick, cut with pastry cutter, place the biscuits on greased tins, and bake in a moderate oven, Gas Mark 5, or 375 deg., for about 15 minutes or until the shortbreads are lightly browned.

Frangipani Slices

For the pastry:

6 oz. self-raising flour	½ egg
3 oz. margarine	little milk to mix
1½ oz. sugar	

For the filling:

3 oz. margarine	2 oz. ground almonds
3 oz. sugar	1 tablespoon cake crumbs
1½ eggs	4 drops almond essence

Mix self-raising flour and sugar for pastry, rub in the margarine, add beaten egg and just sufficient milk to make a firm dough. Roll out fairly thin and line a greased tin—about 10 by 6 by 1 inches. Cream the butter and sugar for the filling, stir in the beaten eggs, ground almonds, cake crumbs and essence. Spread level over the pastry. Bake in a moderately hot oven, Gas Mark 5, or 375 deg., for ½ hour or till pastry is done. When cold, cut into neat slices. *Note.* To vary, reserve a little of the pastry dough, roll out thin, cut into ½-inch wide strips, and lattice the top of the filled sheet before baking.

Shrewsbury Biscuits

2 oz. butter	1 teaspoon cornflour
3 oz. caster sugar	1 teaspoon baking powder
1 egg	grated rind of ½ lemon
6 oz. self-raising flour	milk to mix

Cream the butter and sugar, stir in the beaten egg, gradually stir in the blended flours and baking powder alternating with driblets of milk till a firm dough results, and adding the grated lemon rind last. Roll out about ½ inch thick, cut with a large fluted biscuit cutter, and put the biscuits on lightly greased tins. Bake in a moderately hot oven, Gas Mark 5, or 375 deg., for 12 to 15 minutes or until the biscuits are delicately tinted.

Maw Seed Biscuits

¾ lb. self-raising flour	1 egg
5 oz. caster sugar	3 oz. maw seed
3 oz. butter or margarine	pinch of salt
2 tablespoons olive oil	milk to mix

Mix flour, sugar and salt in a bowl, rub in the butter or margarine. Make a hollow, put in the olive oil and the egg beaten with 3 tablespoons of milk, then mix to a dough, kneading in the maw seeds, and adding just a little more milk if required. Roll out the dough ½ inch thick, cut with 2-inch pastry cutter, place on greased tins, bake in a moderately hot oven, Gas Mark 5, or 375 deg., for 25 minutes. *Note.* Maw seed, so called because it is often found in the maw of birds who are fond of it, is edible poppy seed with an agreeable nutty flavour. It is much used for sprinkling on seeded dinner rolls and fancy bread. The best kind is blue-grey in colour and is known as 'blue maw seed'. It is imported mainly from Holland and is stocked by most corn stores at popular prices.

Nut and Fruit Slices

sweet short crust pastry to line a 9 by 9 inch tin	jam for spreading

For the filling:

4 oz. chopped dates	½ teaspoon cinnamon
1 oz. diced apples or pears	1 oz. ground almonds
1 oz. sultanas	1 oz. caster sugar
1 oz. currants	milk to mix
1 tablespoon brown sugar	

Spread a film of jam on the pastry. Mix all the filling ingredients except the ground almonds, caster sugar and milk, and spread over the jam. Make a paste of the almonds, caster sugar and a little milk, and spread over the fruit. Bake in a moderately hot oven, Gas Mark 5, or 375 deg., for 25 minutes. When cold cut into slices.

Coconut Macaroons (whole egg)

½ lb. fine coconut	2 eggs
6 oz. caster sugar	4 drops vanilla essence

Mix coconut and sugar, add the slightly beaten eggs, add the vanilla essence, mix well. Shape into small cones and place on tins lightly greased and sprinkled with ground rice. Bake about 15 minutes in a moderate oven, Gas Mark 4, or 360 deg.

Coconut Macaroons (whites of egg)

6 oz. medium coconut	2 whites of egg
4 oz. caster sugar	4 drops vanilla essence
1 teaspoon semolina	

Lightly grease a baking sheet and sprinkle a little dry semolina over. Beat the egg whites to a stiff snow. Mix sugar, coconut, semolina and vanilla, then gently fold in the whipped whites. Shape into small, rough pyramids and place on tin. Bake 25 minutes on middle shelf, Gas Mark 3, or 350 deg.

Rolled Oat Flapjacks

$\frac{1}{2}$ lb. rolled oats	1 dessertspoon treacle
2 oz. butter or margarine	pinch of ground cinnamon
2$\frac{1}{2}$ oz. soft brown sugar	pinch of grated lemon rind

Slowly melt the butter or margarine in a saucepan, stir in the sugar, treacle, rolled oats and flavourings. Mix well, and turn into a well-greased baking tin, spreading the mixture about $\frac{1}{2}$ inch thick. Bake in a moderately hot oven, Gas Mark 5, or 375 deg., for 20 minutes. When cold cut into fingers.

Brandy Snap

2 oz. butter	$\frac{1}{4}$ teaspoon ginger
4 oz. brown sugar	$\frac{1}{4}$ teaspoon cinnamon
2 oz. treacle	$\frac{1}{2}$ teaspoon lemon juice
2 oz. flour	

Warm the butter in a saucepan, stir in the sugar, treacle, lemon juice and spices, stir in the flour. Drop teaspoons of the mixture, leaving plenty of space between, on to a greased baking sheet, and bake in a moderate oven, Gas Mark 4, or 360 deg., for about 12 minutes. Take off the snaps with a greased slice, and quickly curl each one round a greased knife handle or similar tool. When set, fill with whipped cream.

Scotch Oat Cakes

1 lb. fresh, medium oatmeal   1 teaspoon salt
2 oz. self-raising flour   milk to mix—about ¼ pint

Mix flour, oatmeal and salt. Add milk gradually and stir until a pliable dough is formed. Cut into pieces weighing 5 oz. each, and roll on a floured board into rounds about 8 inches in diameter; this gives the right thickness. Cut into triangular cakes and place on a greased tin. Bake in a hot oven, Gas Mark 6, or 400 deg., for 15 minutes or till done. *Note.* If the 5-oz. pieces of dough dry quickly, moisten each with a little milk before moulding up.

Afternoon Tea Scones

8 oz. self-raising flour   1 oz. butter
1 heaped teaspoon baking powder   1 oz. sugar
pinch salt   ¼ pint milk

Sift flour, baking powder and salt into a bowl. Make a hollow in the centre and put in the butter, sugar and half the milk. Cream with the hand, add the rest of the milk, and lightly work into a smooth dough. Divide into 4 buns and press each one out gently with the palm of the hand to form thick cakes, slightly higher in the centre. With the back of a knife, cut each cake into 4 scones. Place on a lightly greased and floured tin. Brush with milk. Stand 10 minutes. Bake in a hot oven, Gas Mark 7, or 425 deg., for 12 minutes. To vary, add 2 oz. sultanas and the grated rind of ½ lemon.

Butter Scones

1 lb. plain flour   4 oz. currants
1 oz. baking powder   pinch of salt
4 oz. butter   grated rind of ½ lemon
4 oz. sugar   ¾ pint milk

Sift flour, baking powder and salt into a bowl. Rub in the butter. Make a hollow in the middle, put in the sugar, currants, lemon rind and milk. Mix lightly to dough. Divide into 4 pieces, mould, shape and cut as for Afternoon Tea Scones. Stand 10 minutes, bake in a hot oven, Gas Mark 7, or 425 deg.

American Hot Biscuit (plain scone)

½ lb. self-raising flour
1 teaspoon baking powder
2 oz. butter or margarine

½ teaspoon salt
scant ¼ pint milk and water

Mix flour, salt and baking powder. Rub in butter or margarine. Mix lightly to dough with milk and water. Roll lightly to an oblong sheet about ½ inch thick, fold in half, turn half round, roll and fold once more. Cut with plain cutter into small rounds. Bake on flour-dusted sheets, in a hot oven, Gas Mark 7, or 425 deg., for 12 minutes. Split and butter before serving.

Iced Gingerbread Squares

12 oz. self-raising flour (un-bleached)
2 level teaspoons ginger
1 heaped teaspoon cinnamon
½ teaspoon grated nutmeg
pinch salt
¼ teaspoon bicarbonate of soda

1 egg
4 oz. soft brown sugar
3 oz. margarine
2 tablespoons treacle
2 tablespoons golden syrup
¼ pint milk
water icing

Sift flour, salt and spices into a bowl. Make a hollow and put in the sugar, treacle, syrup, beaten egg, melted margarine and the milk with the soda dissolved in it. Mix well to a smooth batter. Turn into a greased Yorkshire pudding tin; the size supplied with most standard cookers is right. Bake about 1 hour on middle shelf, in a cool oven, Gas Mark 2, or 315 deg. When cold, ice the top with water icing flavoured with lemon juice. Cut into squares when set.

Stuffed Monkey

6 oz. self-raising flour
1 saltspoon bicarbonate of soda
pinch of salt
1 teaspoon ground ginger
½ teaspoon ground nutmeg
½ teaspoon cinnamon

2 oz. soft brown sugar
1 oz. butter
2 tablespoons black treacle
2 tablespoons milk
jam for spreading
2 oz. ground almonds

Mix flour, salt, sugar and spices. Rub in the butter. Make a hollow, put in the treacle and the milk with the soda dissolved in it. Mix to a clear dough. Divide into 2 pieces, and roll, on a well-floured board, into a 10-inch and a 9-inch round. Lift the larger round on to a greased baking tin. Spread it lightly with jam to within an inch of the edge, then cover jam with the ground almonds. Place the smaller round on top. Bring the margin of the lower round well in over the top, and pinch lightly here and there to form a fluted edge. Brush with milk, bake on middle shelf in a slow oven, Gas Mark 3, or 335 deg., for about ½ hour or till deep golden brown. Best eaten cold. *Note.* It is best to make double the amount given in the recipe while one is about it. In this case, add the yolk of an egg to the mix, and a little less milk. Honey is sometimes used in place of jam.

Sticky Parkin

1 lb. medium oatmeal	1 teaspoon ginger
½ lb. flour	1 teaspoon cinnamon
6 oz. margarine	1 teaspoon mixed spice
4 oz. soft brown sugar	½ teaspoon bicarbonate of soda
pinch of salt	milk for top
¾ lb. black treacle	

Mix flour, oatmeal, spices and salt. Rub in the margarine. Warm the treacle and pour in. Dissolve the soda in a little cold milk, and add. Add the sugar. Mix well to a firm dough adding no other liquid. Press the mixture into a well-greased Yorkshire pudding tin. Wash top with milk. Bake, undisturbed, in a very slow oven, Gas Mark 2, or 315 deg., for 2 hours. Take from oven carefully. When cold mark the surface off in squares then break neatly.

Junior Lunch Buns

½ lb. self-raising flour	1 egg
½ oz. cornflour	3 oz. currants
2 teaspoons baking powder	2 oz. cut candied peel
3 oz. sugar	milk to mix
2½ oz. margarine	

Sift flours and baking powder together, rub in the margarine, make a hollow, put in beaten egg, sugar, currants and peel. Mix lightly with just enough milk to make a dough (not a batter). Weigh 1½ pieces of the dough, mould lightly into buns, place on greased tins. Bake in a moderately hot oven, Gas Mark 5, or 380 deg., for 15 minutes or until golden brown.

School Cookies

4 oz. margarine	4 oz. sultanas
5 oz. sugar	½ teaspoon grated lemon rind
12 oz. self-raising flour	milk to mix
1 egg	

Rub the margarine into the flour, stir in the sugar, beaten egg, sultanas, grated lemon rind and sufficient cold milk to make a smooth dough. Roll into walnut size balls, place on greased tins, well-spaced. Bake in a moderately hot oven, Gas Mark 5, or 375 deg., for 25 minutes.

Rock Cakes

1 lb. self-raising flour	3 oz. butter
½ oz. baking powder	4 oz. sugar
1 oz. cornflour	3 oz. currants
1 oz. rice flour	1 egg
pinch of salt	about ⅓ pint milk

Mix flours, baking powder and salt. Rub in the butter. Add beaten egg, sugar, currants and sufficient milk to make a firm dough. Put rocky heaps of the dough on a greased baking sheet and bake in a hot oven, Gas Mark 6, or 400 deg., about 15 minutes.

Raspberry Buns

8 oz. self-raising flour	3 or 4 tablespoons milk
2½ oz. butter	grated rind of ½ lemon
3 oz. sugar	raspberry jam
1 egg	

Rub butter into flour, stir in sugar and lemon rind. Make a hollow, and put in the beaten egg and sufficient milk to make a pliable dough. Flour the hands and roll the dough into a dozen little balls. place on a greased tin with space to expand during baking. Press a small hollow in the top of each with the butt end of an apple corer or similar tool and put in a spoonful of jam. Bake in a moderately hot oven, Gas Mark 5, or 380 deg., for 20 minutes. *Note.* The balls of dough are often rolled into sheets, a spoonful of jam put in the centre, the edges brought up and sealed like money bags, the bag turned upside down and then what was the bottom cut to allow the jam to flow during baking.

Patty Cases (quick method)

3½ oz. self-raising flour   1 teaspoon sugar
2½ oz. butter or margarine   4 tablespoons water

Sift the flour into a bowl. Cut butter or margarine (with the back of a floured knife) into little cubes of hazel nut size, and mix gently into the flour. Put the sugar in the middle. Gradually add the water, mixing lightly to a dough with a fork. *Do not knead.* Let the dough rest 3 minutes. On a flour-dusted board lightly roll the dough into an oblong roughly 10 by 5 inches, and keep the corners square. Fold the oblong in three. Give the pastry a quarter turn, clockwise. Repeat this roll-fold-turn process 4 more times, making 5 times in all. The pastry is then ready for baking. Bake in a hot oven, Gas Mark 8, or 450 deg., for 15 to 20 minutes according to the thickness used for various goods. For Cream Slices, Jam Puffs and Turnovers, roll the pastry ¼ inch thick, dock over with a fork, and bake as directed. For Patty Cases roll pastry about ½ inch thick.

For *Patty Cases* cut the pastry into rounds, and with a cutter two sizes smaller, cut a disc out of half the rounds. Brush the whole rounds with water, put a cut round on each to form patty cases. Brush top with beaten egg, bake as directed; the discs are baked at the same time, and placed on top of the filled patties. Fruits, lemon curd, jam and cream are suitable fillings. For Vol au Vent cases for savoury fillings, omit sugar from the pastry and add, instead, ¼ teaspoon salt. *Note.* To ensure even rising of patty cases, reverse the pastry after cutting, that is, turn the cut pastry upside down.

Hot Water Pie Paste

3 oz. cooking fat   8 oz. flour
¼ pint milk and water   ½ teaspoon salt

Put milk and water in a saucepan, add fat and salt, heat gently till fat is melted. Stir in the flour, and when smooth remove from heat. Knead 2 or 3 minutes. When cold, roll out and line tins. Suitable for most savoury fillings.

Flan Case

Roll out the pastry about ½ inch thick and line a greased flan ring placed on a greased tin. With a fork prick the pastry lightly here and there. Now line the pastry with greased paper, fitting it neatly and so that an inch extends above the edge of the flan ring. Fill the paper with dried peas, haricots or similar ballast. Bake in the usual way but stop the baking a minute or so sooner than ordinary pastry. Take from the oven, carefully remove the paper and ballast, beginning at the edges. Then return the flan to the oven for a minute or two to dry the top, but do not overbake. The flan case is now ready for fruity, cream, or savoury fillings, according to recipe directions. An ordinary Victoria sandwich tin is quite suitable for the baking of a flan case, and, when done, it may remain in the tin until required, or be carefully removed and stored in an airtight tin. Flan Case Pastry recipe below.

Sweet Pastry for Flan Cases and Tarts

10 oz. self-raising flour
3 oz. butter or margarine
3 oz. caster sugar

1 tablespoon salad oil
pinch salt
6 tablespoons cold milk

Mix flour and salt, stir in sugar, rub in butter or margarine with the finger tips. Make a hollow, put in the oil and sufficient milk to make a dough when well-mixed and lightly kneaded. Bake in a moderately hot oven, Gas Mark 5, or 375 deg., for 20 to 25 minutes according to the type of goods.
Note 1. For extra rich pastry, add the yolk of an egg with the oil and use a little less milk. 2. The pastry is good for Mince Pies, Apple Tarts, many kinds of biscuits if an ounce more sugar is added to the ingredients, and for the tops of various baked fruit puddings. For savoury flans, omit the sugar from the pastry and add ½ teaspoon salt.

Short Crust Pastry

½ lb. self-raising flour
¼ teaspoon salt

4 oz. butter or margarine
cold water to mix

Mix flour and salt. Rub in the butter or margarine with the finger tips until the mixture resembles fine bread crumbs. Mix to a stiff paste with about 5 tablespoons cold water (the water required varies according to the flour). Roll out, bake in a hot oven, Gas Mark 7, or 425 deg. Use for tarts, pies, etc.

Fruit and Nut Bread

¾ lb. self-raising flour
1 teaspoon baking powder
1 egg
6 oz. sugar
2 oz. butter or margarine
4 oz. seedless raisins

1 oz. halved glacé cherries
2 oz. currants
1 oz. chopped walnuts or almonds
¼ pint milk
¼ teaspoon salt

Sift flour, salt and baking powder together, rub in the butter or margarine, stir in the sugar. Make a hollow, put in the beaten egg and milk, mix lightly, add the prepared fruits and nuts and knead quickly to dough. Spread it 2 inches deep in a greased tin. Bake in a moderately hot oven, Gas Mark 5, or 375 deg., for about 1¼ hours. When cold, serve thinly sliced and buttered.

HOT PLATE RECIPES

Scotch Pancakes

1½ oz. butter
2½ oz. sugar
1 egg
1 lb. self-raising flour

1 teaspoon baking powder
pinch salt
½ pint milk

Cream the butter, sugar and salt, stir in the beaten egg, gradually stir in the milk, alternating with the blended flour and baking powder. The batter may be mixed in a wide mouthed jug. Pour it on to a slightly greased hot plate or thick frying pan according to the size of pancake wanted. Cook over gentle heat to brown both sides lightly, lifting the pancakes with a slice when bubbles begin to appear.

American Hot Cakes

6 tablespoons self-raising flour
3 tablespoons buckwheat flour or fine 'oven-dried bread raspings'
2 teaspoons baking powder

1 egg
¼ teaspoon salt
¼ pint milk
¼ pint water

Put the dry ingredients in a jug, stir in the beaten egg, gradually add half the milk and water, add the rest of the liquid gradually. Stir well to form a thick, creamy batter. Pour tablespoons of the batter on to a greased hot plate leaving space for the cakes to flow. Cook gently about 4 minutes, turn to cook the other side 3 minutes. Serve hot with syrup, treacle or honey. About 1 dozen cakes.

Yorkshire Riddle Cakes

1 lb. fine fresh oatmeal
½ oz. flour
½ oz. fresh yeast

1 level teaspoon salt
water to mix

Mix flour, oatmeal and salt in a bowl. Dissolve yeast in a spoonful of warm water and put in the centre. Add lukewarm water and

139

stir till a cream-like batter results. Pour a long strip of batter on to a warmed girdle, bakestone or frying pan. The cakes puff up at once and acquire a roughish top with a smooth base. Cook gently 2 minutes. Hang the cakes on a paper-covered line to dry for a day or two, then crisp in the oven for a few minutes before serving with butter spread all over them. *Note.* 'Riddle' is probably a West Riding version of girdle.

Welsh Bakestone Gems

4 oz. self-raising flour
1 teaspoon baking powder
pinch salt
2 teaspoons sugar

1 dessertspoon cut peel
1 oz. butter
milk to mix

Mix flour, baking powder and salt, rub in butter, stir in sugar and finely cut candied lemon peel, mix with a little milk to smooth, firm dough. Roll ¼ inch thick, cut with a 2-inch pastry cutter into rounds, bake on a bakestone over gentle heat, turning to cook both sides lightly. Serve hot.

Potato Farls

1½ lb. floury mashed potato
4 oz. self-raising flour

2 oz. butter
¼ teaspoon salt

Rub butter into flour and salt, blend with potato, roll out ½ inch thick on a floured board, cut 6-inch rounds into quarters, bake both sides on a hot plate. Serve hot, split and buttered.

Hot Plate Currant Scones

½ lb. self-raising flour
1 teaspoon baking powder
1 oz. butter

1 oz. currants
pinch salt
milk to mix

Mix flour, powder and salt, rub in butter, add milk sufficient to make a soft dough, work in the cleaned currants, roll out on a floured board ½ inch thick. Cut 5-inch rounds into quarters, bake both sides lightly on a greased hot plate, turning after one side has cooked for 3 minutes.

Wheatmeal Pancakes

4 oz. wholewheat flour	1 egg
2 oz. self-raising flour	milk to mix
pinch salt	1 teaspoon melted butter

Mix flours and salt, stir in beaten egg, add milk gradually and stir till batter is the consistency of thick cream. Then stir in the melted butter. Pour, from a jug for preference, small round patches on to a greased hot plate. Turn after 1 minute to brown the other side.

SANDWICHES, PASTES AND SPREADS

Savoury Sandwich Spread

4 oz. grated cheese
1 dessertspoon grated onion
½ oz. butter
2 tablespoons grated tomato

1 teaspoon made mustard
pinch ground cinnamon
1 tablespoon evaporated milk

Cream the butter, mix with the remaining ingredients. Spread thickly in brown bread sandwiches. Good as a stuffing for roasted potatoes.

Curd Cheese Sandwich Spread

4 oz. curd cheese
4 tablespoons unsweetened
    evaporated milk, or cream
1 teaspoon onion juice
1 tablespoon minced cucumber

1 teaspoon made mustard
2 teaspoons minced gherkin
pepper, salt and nutmeg to
    taste

Stir onion juice into milk or cream, stir in the curd cheese, add the rest of the ingredients and mix well.

Hot Savoury Spread

1 cup boiled rice
1 cup thick white sauce
1 tablespoon peanut butter
1 tablespoon tomato sauce

1 teaspoon grated raw onion
½ teaspoon yeast extract
1 oz. grated cheese
pepper and salt to taste

Put peanut butter and extract in a saucepan, add a dessertspoon boiling water and stir over gentle heat till dissolved. Mix in the remaining ingredients and cook gently for 2 minutes more. Use hot. Nice cold as a sandwich spread. Mixed with a beaten egg, the spread may be baked in a sharp oven, cut into squares and served hot with gravy.

Celery Cheese Spread

4 oz. grated cheese   1 teaspoon celery salt
1 tablespoon grated celery   ½ oz. butter

Cream the butter, blend with the grated cheese, grated celery and celery salt.

Egg and Lentil Paste

1 cup cooked red lentils   a grate of garlic
yolks of 2 hard-boiled eggs   pinch each: nutmeg, pepper and
1 oz. cream cheese   salt

Cream the cheese with the seasonings and the yolks of the eggs, blend with the lentils, pound very smooth. A rich spread for bread. If the whites of the eggs are chopped fine with a little cress, they make an attractive sandwich filling.

Curd Cheese and Tomato Cream

4 oz. fresh curd cheese   4 oz. tomatoes
½ oz. butter   pepper and salt
1 teaspoon grated onion   pinch of paprika

Peel the tomatoes and pass through a sieve, blend with the curd cheese and seasonings. Cream the butter and gradually add the tomato-cheese. Mash very smooth. Sprinkle a pinch of paprika over the cream.

Curried Lentil Spread

1 cup cooked red lentils   ½ cup curry sauce (see p. 25)
1 hard-boiled egg   dry bread crumbs

Grate the hard-boiled egg, mix with the sieved lentils and the sauce, add sufficient bread crumbs to make a firm paste, pound very smooth, fill into small pots, run melted butter over. A tasty tea-time spread.

Haricot Tomato Paste

1 cup baked beans in tomato   1 oz. cream cheese
  sauce   fine dry bread raspings
½ oz. butter

Sieve the beans, cream the butter, mash the cheese smooth. Mix the ingredients with sufficient bread raspings (grated from the crust of a well-baked loaf) to make a paste of spreading consistency. A savoury spread for home-made wholewheat bread.

Savoury Walnut Spread

2 oz. ground walnuts
1 cup cooked rice
yolk of 1 hard-boiled egg

½ teaspoon celery salt
1 teaspoon grated onion
½ teaspoon yeast extract

Mix the ingredients to a smooth paste then pass through a sieve or fine strainer. Nice as a sandwich filling or as a relish with Spanish onions baked in a well-buttered dish.

Peanut Butter Spread

2 oz. peanut butter
1 tablespoon fried chopped onion

1 cup bread crumbs
1 tablespoon evaporated milk

Add the milk to the peanut butter, warm slightly if the butter is very firm, make smooth, add the remaining ingredients. Pass through a sieve. Spread on bread and add a little finely chopped cress for a satisfying sandwich.

Dutch Cheese Sandwich

Mix a dessertspoon each of finely chopped sauerkraut and finely chopped black olives, butter 2 thin slices of Gouda cheese and sandwich them with the filling, put the cheese sandwich between thin slices of wholemeal bread and butter. To vary, use rye bread.

Poached Egg Sandwich

Poach the egg so that the yolk is rather firm, chop fine, mix with the same amount of grated raw carrot and a dessertspoon of mayonnaise, with a good dash of pepper in the seasoning.

Salad Sandwich

Finely chop and shred equal parts of lettuce, raw cabbage, fresh parsley, tomato and apple, bind with thick mayonnaise dressing. Thin, flexible slices of buttered bread will be required to hold the filling.

Various Sandwich Fillings

1. Chopped egg, asparagus tips, mayonnaise.
2. Grated cooked beet, grated onion, grated cheese, all mixed with creamed butter.
3. Grated cheese, grated celery, finely minced onion.
4. Cream cheese, sliced pear, mayonnaise.
5. Chopped cress, tomato, cucumber.
6. Mashed ripe banana blended with creamed butter.
7. Sliced bananas and grated chocolate, creamed, between very thin brown bread and butter.
8. Cream cheese, finely chopped apple and celery.
9. Sliced nutmeat, mustard, chopped hard-boiled egg, creamed butter.
10. Cold scrambled egg, sliced olive, tomato.
11. Cream Danish blue cheese and mix with equal amounts of grated Cheddar, and curd or cream cheese, creamed butter. Add a dab of made mustard.
12. Cream cheese, chopped walnuts, finely minced parsley.
13. Cold Spanish Omelet (onion and tomato) (see p. 104).
14. Flaked cheese, minced dates, ground walnuts creamed together with butter.

Avocado and Egg Sandwich

Slice the avocado thinly, sprinkle oil and lemon juice over, stand 10 minutes. Mix with finely chopped hard-boiled egg, seasoned to taste and use generously as sandwich filling.

Danish Cheese Sandwich

Cream Danish blue cheese, blend with finely chopped pickled cucumber, mix with creamed butter, spread between slices of rye bread.

Lentil Roast Sandwich

Sliced lentil roast, dabbed with a little made mustard, makes a hearty sandwich filling.

Curried Nutmeat Sandwich

Pass ½ cup rich Curry Sauce through the strainer, blend with 1 cup mashed nutmeat, adding a spoonful of chopped capers. Use for 3-decker sandwiches, one of the fillings being finely chopped salad, the other, blended Curry Sauce and nutmeat. (A good way of using left overs.)

Savoury Sandwich

Many cooked savouries are good as sandwich fillings. Cream 1 cup cold savoury with 1 teaspoon butter, a dessertspoon chutney or tomato sauce, and seasoning to taste. For a richer filling add a grated hard-boiled egg.

Creamed Vegetable Sandwich

Combine ½ cup each freshly grated raw carrot, finely shredded raw cabbage and finely chopped cress, with ½ cup sour cream. *Note.* Unsweetened evaporated milk thickened with lemon juice can replace sour cream.

AGAR JELLIES

Agar Jellies

2 rounded teaspoons powdered   1 pint boiling water
New Zealand Agar   2 tablespoons cold water

Put the powdered New Zealand agar in a basin, add the cold water, stir, let stand 10 minutes. Pour on the boiling water, stir, boil 1 minute, stir well.
This jelly will set within ½ hour of preparation. It may be reboiled without losing its jellying power, and differs in this respect from ordinary jelly. When the jelly has cooled slightly, seasoning, sweetening, and the ingredients to be jellied may be added, such as diced cooked vegetables, nutmeat, diced savouries, hard-boiled egg, sliced gherkin and so on. Pour into wetted moulds and stand till set. *Note.* Agar jellies are not so clear as ordinary jelly. Dark-coloured extracts added to the clear jelly will further lower the clarity and should therefore be used sparingly.

Café Au Lait Jellies

Follow the recipe for Agar Jellies but, instead of boiling water, add 1 pint strong milk coffee sweetened with 1 oz. sugar and strained twice.

Orange and Lemon Jellies

Follow the recipe for Agar Jellies, but instead of boiling water, add 1 pint boiling fruit juices and water, sweetened to taste before boiling. About ⅓ each: water, orange juice and lemon juice is a good proportion.

Chocolate Cream Jellies

Blend ½ pint Agar Jelly (see recipe for Agar Jellies) with ½ pint double thick Chocolate Blanc Mange, and pour into moulds. When set, unmould and add a whirl of whipped cream before serving. *Note.* For Chocolate Blanc Mange follow instructions on the packet and vary as required.

147

Jellied Fruits

Pour 1 pint sweetened lemon Agar Jelly into a shallow dish to a depth of ¾ inch. When cooled but not yet set, add 2 cups fruits such as diced pineapple, pear, glacé cherries, strawberries, etc. When firmly set, pour on 1 pint jellied custard, cooled before adding. Cut into squares when set, decorate with made cream or whipped cream, flaked chocolate and chopped nuts. *Note.* To prepare jellied custard, make the custard double the usual thickness and boil 1 minute with 1 level dessertspoon soaked agar.

Savoury Jelly

Follow the recipe for Agar Jellies, and before turning the finished jelly into the moulds, stir in a pinch of salt, a very tiny dash of pepper, and one-tenth of a teaspoon of yeast extract. If required for coating savouries, use rather less than the stated amount of water. For white coating jelly, use milk, or thin White Sauce, instead of water.

CHRISTMAS FAVOURITES

Christmas Roast

½ lb. red lentils	2 eggs
4 oz. vermicelli	½ lb. onions
½ lb. flaked cheese	3 oz. vegetarian cooking fat
4 oz. wholemeal bread crumbs	2 bay leaves
1 clove garlic	½ teaspoon mixed dried herbs
grate of nutmeg	1 teaspoon salt

Finely chop onions and brown slowly in fat. Put washed lentils in saucepan with bay leaves and ½ pint cold water, boil up, simmer 25 minutes, stirring occasionally. Remove bay leaves. Boil vermicelli in 1 quart water 7 minutes. Grate garlic. Beat eggs. Thoroughly mix all the prepared ingredients, pack the mixture 3 inches deep in a well-buttered baking dish. Bake 45 minutes in a moderately hot oven, Gas Mark 5, or 375 deg. Serve hot with thickened brown gravy, potatoes, peas and cauliflower or other preferred vegetables.

Christmas Nutmeat (Steamed)

¼ lb. ground almonds	1 clove garlic
¼ lb. ground Brazil nuts	1 teaspoon salt
2 cups cooked rice	pinch each: pepper, mace and
1 cup wholemeal bread crumbs	nutmeg
3 eggs	½ teaspoon dried thyme
1 teaspoon yeast extract	2 oz. cooking fat
4 onions	

Slowly fry chopped onions till golden brown. Grate the garlic. Beat the eggs. Dissolve extract in a tablespoon of hot water. Mix all the prepared ingredients thoroughly and turn into 1 or 2 greased pudding basins or similar moulds, cover with buttered paper, steam 1½ hours. Stand 3 minutes, unmould on to a hot platter. Serve hot with thick gravy, mushroom sauce, baked potatoes, sprouts and buttered carrots. *Note.* For the Mushroom Sauce, stir 2 oz. chopped cooked mushrooms into ¾ pint White Sauce just before serving.

Stuffed Nut Roast

½ lb. ground mixed nuts	1 hard-boiled egg
1 cup fried onions	1 cup cooked rice
2 eggs	1 oz. grated cheese
2 cups bread crumbs	seasoning
2 shredded wheat sections	

Crush the shredded wheat fine with a rolling pin. Beat the eggs. Mix nuts, breadcrumbs, seasoning, shredded wheat, fried onions and beaten eggs, and divide the mixture in two. Grate the hard-boiled egg and mix with the grated cheese and cooked rice to a firm stuffing, adding seasoning to taste. Spread half the nut mixture in a buttered pie dish, spread the stuffing over it. Spread the remaining nutmeat mixture on top, dot with butter, bake in a moderate oven for 45 minutes. Serve hot with Tomato Gravy and vegetables. (For Tomato Gravy see p. 50.)

Christmas Pudding

6 oz. sultanas	4 oz. soft brown sugar
6 oz. currants	4 oz. grated fat
6 oz. raisins	3 eggs
4 oz. grated apple	grated rind of a lemon
1 tablespoon marmalade	2 teaspoons mixed spice
2 oz. brown bread crumbs	1 teaspoon cinnamon
1 oz. ground almonds	pinch of salt
1 tablespoon black treacle	

Clean the fruit, dry and dust with flour. Beat the eggs. Mix all the ingredients thoroughly, stand 1 hour, then stir again. Turn the mixture into 2 well-greased medium pudding basins and cover with greased paper, then with scalded and well-wrung cloths. Steam 4 hours. Stand 5 minutes before unmoulding. This pudding may be cooked 3 days before it is required; to re-heat, steam 1½ hours. Serve with sauce.

Rum Sauce

Mix ½ pint thin Custard Sauce with ¼ pint cream, add a tablespoon sugar, and heat very gently without boiling. Just before serving, stir in 3 tablespoons rum, or a little rum essence to taste.

Christmas Salad

1 cup diced pears	1 cup sliced celery
1 cup diced apples	1 cup sliced chicory
½ cup sliced gherkins	1 cup diced hard-boiled egg
½ cup seedless raisins	½ cup grated raw carrot
watercress	French dressing

Reserve the cress for garnishing. Mix the rest of the salad ingredients carefully, adding the freshly grated carrot last, and the dressing rather freely. Mix the salad at the very last convenient moment. Cheese of the blue types will be good with it.

Christmas Cake

½ lb. butter	1 lb. currants
6 oz. soft brown sugar	4 oz. cut candied peel
4 eggs	2 oz. halved glacé cherries
¾ lb. self-raising flour	2 oz. chopped almonds
juice of 1 lemon	1 teaspoon mixed spice
grated rind of ½ lemon	½ teaspoon ground mace
1 dessertspoon black treacle	4 tablespoons milk
1 lb. sultanas	

Cream the butter, add the sugar and cream again. Beat in the treacle. Beat in the eggs singly. Stir in the blended flour and spices in several lots, alternating with driblets of milk. Add the lemon juice and rind, the chopped nuts and the cleaned and flour-dusted fruits. Put the batter in greased tins doubly lined with greased paper. Bake in a slow oven, Gas Mark 3, or 335 deg., for about 3 hours. When required, the cake may be covered with Almond Paste (see p. 152), iced and decorated.

Marzipan without Almonds

2 oz. butter	½ lb. plain cake crumbs
2 oz. caster sugar	2 teaspoons almond essence

Cream the butter very light, add the sugar and cream again, stir in the cake crumbs and the essence. Knead well to a smooth round disc the size of the cake top. Brush the cake top with warmed, clear jam, and turn it on to the marzipan which should be on a sugar sprinkled board. Use a tumbler to press the edge of the marzipan level with the cake.

Almond Paste

8 oz. ground almonds   1 egg
4 oz. caster sugar   2 teaspoons lemon juice
4 oz. icing sugar

Beat the egg slightly. Pass the sugars through a sieve into a bowl. Stir in the ground almonds. Add the lemon juice. Gradually stir in the slightly beaten egg, bearing in mind that the whole of it may not be required. Mix to a firm paste, turn on to a sugar sprinkled board and knead well till very smooth and pliable, adding very little more egg if necessary.

Royal Icing

½ lb. icing sugar   white of 1 egg
juice of ½ lemon

Sift the icing sugar, add the unbeaten white of the egg gradually to the sugar, add lemon juice by degrees, stirring to a thick paste. Add a little more lemon juice if necessary, Beat the icing quickly for several minutes. It should be light and thick. Use as required.

Mince Pies

1 lb. self-raising flour   1 large egg
½ lb. butter and margarine (in   2 oz. caster sugar
     any proportion)   1 oz. soft brown sugar
pinch of salt   milk to mix

Mix flour and salt, rub in the butter and margarine, stir in the sugars. Make a hollow, put in the slightly beaten egg and a tablespoon of milk and mix to a pliable dough with no more milk than is necessary. To make pies, roll out the dough ¼ inch thick on a floured board, and cut to rounds of desired size with pastry cutter. Put a spoonful of mincemeat in the centre of each of half the rounds, brush edges with milk, fix on the top rounds. With the edge of a cup ¼ inch smaller than the pastry rounds, press on top to form border and seal. (Dip cup edge in flour repeatedly.) Bake in a moderately hot oven, Gas Mark 5, or 380 deg., for 20 minutes. Sprinkle sugar on before serving.

MISCELLANEOUS RECIPES

Lemon Curd

2 lemons   4 oz. butter
½ lb. lump sugar   2 eggs

Score the lemons with the prongs of a fork, rub several sugar lumps on the broken rind to take up the flavour. Slowly melt the butter in a saucepan, stir in the juice of the lemons, add the prepared sugar, cook gently till the sugar dissolves. Now cook for 3 minutes more. Remove from heat, cool a little, gradually stir in the beaten eggs, cook over hot water (double pan), stirring constantly, till thickened (5 or 6 minutes). Jar when cold. A filling for lemon cheese tarts, and an attractive tea-time spread.

Mincemeat

¼ lb. seedless raisins   ½ teaspoon grated nutmeg
¼ lb. sultanas   1 teaspoon cinnamon
¼ lb. currants   4 oz. soft brown sugar
½ lb. apples   grated rind and juice of 1 lemon
2 oz. mixed candied peel   pinch salt
4 oz. grated hard nut fat

Chop the cored, peeled apples fine, chop raisins, peel and sultanas together, or pass through mincer. Clean the currants particularly well, and leave whole. Mix all the ingredients and press into jars. Seal and store in a cool place. This makes about 3 lb. mincemeat, good for puddings and pies.

Black Currant Tea

Pour 1 pint boiling water over a pinch of tea, strain off immediately, stir a heaped tablespoon home made black currant jam and a dessertspoon lemon juice into the strained liquid. Serve very hot, on cold evenings.

Beet and Lemon Conserve

1 lb. boiled beet
2 medium lemons
¼ pint water
1¼ lb. lump sugar

2 oz. hazel nuts
1 teaspoon ginger
pinch cinnamon

Wash the lemons, slice very thinly, put them in a saucepan with the water, boil up, simmer 15 minutes. Add the sugar, stir over moderate heat till dissolved, add the beets cut into 2-inch sticks the thickness of macaroni. Boil up again, cook 20 minutes, add the ginger and cinnamon and the lightly roasted hazel nuts, and boil 15 minutes more. Store when cold in sealed jars. Delicious with thick cream or with brown bread and butter.

Grapefruit and Lemon Marmalade

Formula: to each ½ lb. citrus fruit
    add—⅚ pint of water
    and—1 lb. 6 oz. sugar

Method: Wash the fruits, cover them, whole, with water, simmer very gently 4 hours, adding boiling water to keep fruits well covered as necessary. Drain off and keep the cooking water. When cool, slice the fruits very thinly with a sharp knife on a stout board, keeping the escaping juice. Now measure all the cooking water and juice, and make up to ⅚ pint for each ½ lb. of original fruit weighed when raw. Add cut, cooked fruit to water, put in a bowl and let stand 12 hours. Add 1 lb. 6 oz. sugar for each ½ lb. of raw fruit, simmer till sugar is dissolved, bring to boil, boil for 25 to 40 minutes, according to acidity and pectin value of the fruit. Test in a saucer in the usual way, and when the marmalade is done, turn into warm, dry jars. *Note.* A quarter of the fruit should be lemon. The formula, however, is equally good for Lemon Marmalade consisting entirely of lemons. It is also good for Seville bitter oranges with lemon as directed.

Vejisavs

3 cups mashed potato
2 oz. ground almonds
2 oz. cream cheese
1 egg
1 tablespoon tomato purée

1 tablespoon grated onion
1 teaspoon salt
a pinch each: pepper, nutmeg and
    mixed dried herbs
1 cup soft bread crumbs

Cream the cheese with the onion and tomato, add the beaten egg gradually, stir in the ground almonds, herbs, spices and seasonings, mix in the mashed potato and bread crumbs. Shape the mixture into small cakes or sausages and bake on a well-greased tin in a hot oven, turning to cook both sides, or fry in deep hot fat till golden brown. Serve hot with peas, tomatoes and fried onions, or cold with salad.

Frying Batter (1)

4 oz. flour	2 teaspoons salad oil
1 egg	¼ pint water
1 teaspoon lemon juice	pinch of salt

Sift flour and salt together, stir in oil and beaten yolk of egg, gradually add the water and lemon juice. Stand the batter for a few minutes, then, just before using, fold in the stiffly whipped white of the egg. *Note.* For coating sweet fritters, add a pinch of sugar and cinnamon to the batter.

Frying Batter (2)

4 oz. self-raising flour	white of an egg
½ oz. melted butter	pinch of salt
¼ pint water	

Sift flour and salt together, make a hollow, gradually put in the blended butter and slightly warmed water, while stirring to a smooth batter. Fold in the stiffly frothed white of the egg. Use as required.

Home Made Baking Powder

Sift together 2 oz. cream of tartar and 1 oz. bicarbonate of soda, mix well and sift again. Store in a covered jar and keep jar in an airtight tin. This is the best kind of baking powder for all baking purposes. The ingredients are best bought from the largest multiple chemists. The cost is slightly less than that of proprietary baking powders.

Cold Galantine (1)

¼ lb. mushrooms	1 cup cooked rice
6 oz. onions	1 cup bread crumbs
2 oz. ground almonds	1 teaspoon salt
2 eggs	pinch each: pepper, herbs and
1 oz. butter	nutmeg

Slice the mushrooms, chop onions, stew both together with the butter and a little water till tender. Beat the eggs with the seasonings and herbs. Thoroughly mix all the ingredients, pack in a buttered casserole, bake in a moderate oven, middle shelf, Gas Mark 5, or 375 deg., for 1 hour. When quite cold, slice and serve with salad, wholewheat rolls and butter. *Note.* Two or three hard-boiled eggs, whole or halved, may be put in the centre of the mixture before baking, if egg galantine is wanted.

Cold Galantine (2)

4 oz. ground almonds	1 cup fried onions
2 oz. ground walnuts	1 cup diced peeled tomatoes
6 oz. bread crumbs	1 teaspoon salt
½ teaspoon mixed dried herbs	dash each: pepper and nutmeg
2 eggs	

Beat the eggs, mix all the ingredients, turn into a buttered mould, cover with greased paper, steam 1½ hours. Stand 5 minutes, unmould carefully, stand till quite cold. Slice and serve with egg mayonnaise, green salad, brown bread and butter.

Yorkshire Pudding

4 oz. plain flour	1 oz. butter or fat
1 level teaspoon salt	½ pint milk
1 egg	1 tablespoon water

Sift flour and salt into a mixing bowl. Make a hollow. Break in the egg. Add the water. Stir and beat to a smooth batter, adding the milk gradually. Beat for 2 minutes. Make the butter or fat very hot in the Yorkshire Pudding tin, pour in the batter, and bake about 20 minutes in a moderately hot oven, Gas Mark 6, or 400 deg. Cut into squares and serve hot. Good either with rich gravy, or a sprinkling of sugar.

Pancakes

Use the same ingredients as for Yorkshire Pudding and prepare the batter as directed above. Pour a film of the batter into a greased frying pan, cook 2 minutes, toss or turn, cook the other side. Gentle heat is required. Keep the pancakes hot until all are done. Roll up; serve with sugar and cut lemon. *Note.* For the savoury

dish known as Kromeskis, cook the pancakes on one side only, put a spoonful of any savoury filling in the centre, fold into 'packets', preferably of triangular shape, then fry in hot fat. (See p. 40.)

Welsh Rarebit

6 oz. Cheddar cheese	1 level teaspoon made mustard
½ oz. butter	pinch pepper
1 tablespoon milk	hot buttered toast

Melt butter in a saucepan, add milk, stir in mustard and pepper, stir in the diced cheese. Cook and stir over moderate heat until the cheese is melted. Pour on to the hot toast and serve immediately. To vary: stir in a teaspoon of fine bread crumbs along with the diced cheese; this gives the rarebit a pleasant texture.

SOME CULINARY HERBS

Bay Leaf. Imparts a modified almond flavour to custards, milk puddings, and certain sweet dishes. Simmered with lentils it improves flavour. One of the essential ingredients of the Herb Bouquet or Bouquet Garni which consists of parsley, thyme and bay leaf.

Chervil. Used in same way as parsley for flavouring soups, savouries and salads. An attractive garnish.

Chives. Useful when subdued onion flavour is required. Good for salads and for adding to dishes cooked *au gratin*.

Garlic. Of great value in savoury dishes. It is less pungent when finely minced and gently fried along with onions. Small amounts are best measured by grating a clove of garlic on a modern grater. A small section of the garlic bulb is called a 'clove'. A cut clove of garlic rubbed round the salad bowl imparts sufficient flavour to the contents of the salad. Sliced bread for sandwiches may be treated in the same way when the savoury fillings require piquancy. Garlic improves most vegetable soups and lentil dishes.

Marjoram. Of the various kinds, the sweet or knotted kind is most used for mixing with other herbs, and for savoury stuffings.

Mint. Shredded fresh mint is good in salads, sprinkled over cooked potatoes, and as an ingredient of savouries containing peas, beans or lentils. A couple of fresh mint leaves in a tumbler of very weak, lemon-flavoured tea, milkless, of course, enhance the flavour. A sprig of fresh mint added to garden peas after they are cooked, is sufficient for the flavour required. This also applies to new potatoes. Older vegetables are improved by addition of the shredded leaf. Shredded mint in lemon juice makes an attractive mint sauce.

Parsley. Valuable for garnishing, as an ingredient of salads, savouries and soups, and as an ingredient of the herb bouquet, stuffings and sauces.

Sage. Best mixed with onion and other herbs in stuffings and savouries.

Shallot. Useful for imparting delicate onion flavour to savouries, salads, soups and stuffings.

Tarragon. Used for flavouring vinegar, lemon juice, certain sauces and soups.

Thyme. Both the Common and Lemon varieties are good in rissoles and stuffings, and as an ingredient of the Bouquet Garni.

OVEN TEMPERATURES

GAS MARK NUMBER	approximating to	CENTRE OVEN TEMPERATURE
		Fahrenheit
1	. . . .	290 Degrees
SLOW { 2	. . . .	315 ,,
3	. . . .	335 ,,
MODERATE { 4	. . . .	360 ,,
MODERATELY { 5	. . . .	380 ,,
HOT { 6	. . . .	400 ,,
HOT { 7	. . . .	425 ,,
8	. . . .	445 ,,

(i)   In all ovens the upper part is the hotter.

(ii) In electric ovens the dial numbers indicate the temperature directly, e.g. No. 2 gives 200 deg. F., No. 3 gives 300 deg. F. and so on.

(iii) The above table applies to the more widely distributed types of gas cooker.

INDEX

The recipes provide sufficient for 4 to 6 portions except where otherwise stated

Wholewheat Bread, Cakes and Puddings

A CATALOGUE OF SELECTED DOVER BOOKS
IN ALL FIELDS OF INTEREST

A CATALOGUE OF SELECTED DOVER
BOOKS IN ALL FIELDS OF INTEREST

CELESTIAL OBJECTS FOR COMMON TELESCOPES, T. W. Webb. The most used book in amateur astronomy: inestimable aid for locating and identifying nearly 4,000 celestial objects. Edited, updated by Margaret W. Mayall. 77 illustrations. Total of 645pp. 5⅜ x 8½.
20917-2, 20918-0 Pa., Two-vol. set $9.00

HISTORICAL STUDIES IN THE LANGUAGE OF CHEMISTRY, M. P. Crosland. The important part language has played in the development of chemistry from the symbolism of alchemy to the adoption of systematic nomenclature in 1892. ". . . wholeheartedly recommended,"—Science. 15 illustrations. 416pp. of text. 5⅝ x 8¼. 63702-6 Pa. $6.00

BURNHAM'S CELESTIAL HANDBOOK, Robert Burnham, Jr. Thorough, readable guide to the stars beyond our solar system. Exhaustive treatment, fully illustrated. Breakdown is alphabetical by constellation: Andromeda to Cetus in Vol. 1; Chamaeleon to Orion in Vol. 2; and Pavo to Vulpecula in Vol. 3. Hundreds of illustrations. Total of about 2000pp. 6⅛ x 9¼.
23567-X, 23568-8, 23673-0 Pa., Three-vol. set $27.85

THEORY OF WING SECTIONS: INCLUDING A SUMMARY OF AIR-FOIL DATA, Ira H. Abbott and A. E. von Doenhoff. Concise compilation of subatomic aerodynamic characteristics of modern NASA wing sections, plus description of theory. 350pp. of tables. 693pp. 5⅜ x 8½.
60586-8 Pa. $8.50

DE RE METALLICA, Georgius Agricola. Translated by Herbert C. Hoover and Lou H. Hoover. The famous Hoover translation of greatest treatise on technological chemistry, engineering, geology, mining of early modern times (1556). All 289 original woodcuts. 638pp. 6¾ x 11.
60006-8 Clothbd. $17.95

THE ORIGIN OF CONTINENTS AND OCEANS, Alfred Wegener. One of the most influential, most controversial books in science, the classic statement for continental drift. Full 1966 translation of Wegener's final (1929) version. 64 illustrations. 246pp. 5⅜ x 8½. 61708-4 Pa. $4.50

THE PRINCIPLES OF PSYCHOLOGY, William James. Famous long course complete, unabridged. Stream of thought, time perception, memory, experimental methods; great work decades ahead of its time. Still valid, useful; read in many classes. 94 figures. Total of 1391pp. 5⅜ x 8½.
20381-6, 20382-4 Pa., Two-vol. set $13.00

DRAWINGS OF WILLIAM BLAKE, William Blake. 92 plates from Book of Job, *Divine Comedy, Paradise Lost,* visionary heads, mythological figures, Laocoon, etc. Selection, introduction, commentary by Sir Geoffrey Keynes. 178pp. 8⅛ x 11. 22303-5 Pa. $4.00

ENGRAVINGS OF HOGARTH, William Hogarth. 101 of Hogarth's greatest works: *Rake's Progress, Harlot's Progress, Illustrations for Hudibras, Before and After, Beer Street and Gin Lane,* many more. Full commentary. 256pp. 11 x 13¾. 22479-1 Pa. $12.95

DAUMIER: 120 GREAT LITHOGRAPHS, Honore Daumier. Wide-ranging collection of lithographs by the greatest caricaturist of the 19th century. Concentrates on eternally popular series on lawyers, on married life, on liberated women, etc. Selection, introduction, and notes on plates by Charles F. Ramus. Total of 158pp. 9⅜ x 12¼. 23512-2 Pa. $6.00

DRAWINGS OF MUCHA, Alphonse Maria Mucha. Work reveals drafts-man of highest caliber: studies for famous posters and paintings, render-ings for book illustrations and ads, etc. 70 works, 9 in color; including 6 items not drawings. Introduction. List of illustrations. 72pp. 9⅜ x 12¼. (Available in U.S. only) 23672-2 Pa. $4.00

GIOVANNI BATTISTA PIRANESI: DRAWINGS IN THE PIERPONT MORGAN LIBRARY, Giovanni Battista Piranesi. For first time ever all of Morgan Library's collection, world's largest. 167 illustrations of rare Piranesi drawings—archeological, architectural, decorative and visionary. Essay, detailed list of drawings, chronology, captions. Edited by Felice Stampfle. 144pp. 9⅜ x 12¼. 23714-1 Pa. $7.50

NEW YORK ETCHINGS (1905-1949), John Sloan. All of important American artist's N.Y. life etchings. 67 works include some of his best art; also lively historical record—Greenwich Village, tenement scenes. Edited by Sloan's widow. Introduction and captions. 79pp. 8⅜ x 11¼. 23651-X Pa. $4.00

CHINESE PAINTING AND CALLIGRAPHY: A PICTORIAL SURVEY, Wan-go Weng. 69 fine examples from John M. Crawford's matchless private collection: landscapes, birds, flowers, human figures, etc., plus calligraphy. Every basic form included: hanging scrolls, handscrolls, album leaves, fans, etc. 109 illustrations. Introduction. Captions. 192pp. 8⅞ x 11¾. 23707-9 Pa. $7.95

DRAWINGS OF REMBRANDT, edited by Seymour Slive. Updated Lipp-mann, Hofstede de Groot edition, with definitive scholarly apparatus. All portraits, biblical sketches, landscapes, nudes, Oriental figures, classical studies, together with selection of work by followers. 550 illustrations. Total of 630pp. 9⅛ x 12¼. 21485-0, 21486-9 Pa., Two-vol. set $15.00

THE DISASTERS OF WAR, Francisco Goya. 83 etchings record horrors of Napoleonic wars in Spain and war in general. Reprint of 1st edition, plus 3 additional plates. Introduction by Philip Hofer. 97pp. 9⅜ x 8¼. 21872-4 Pa. $4.00

THE SENSE OF BEAUTY, George Santayana. Masterfully written discussion of nature of beauty, materials of beauty, form, expression; art, literature, social sciences all involved. 168pp. 5⅜ x 8½. 20238-0 Pa. $3.00

ON THE IMPROVEMENT OF THE UNDERSTANDING, Benedict Spinoza. Also contains *Ethics, Correspondence*, all in excellent R. Elwes translation. Basic works on entry to philosophy, pantheism, exchange of ideas with great contemporaries. 402pp. 5⅜ x 8½. 20250-X Pa. $4.50

THE TRAGIC SENSE OF LIFE, Miguel de Unamuno. Acknowledged masterpiece of existential literature, one of most important books of 20th century. Introduction by Madariaga. 367pp. 5⅜ x 8½.
20257-7 Pa. $4.50

THE GUIDE FOR THE PERPLEXED, Moses Maimonides. Great classic of medieval Judaism attempts to reconcile revealed religion (Pentateuch, commentaries) with Aristotelian philosophy. Important historically, still relevant in problems. Unabridged Friedlander translation. Total of 473pp. 5⅜ x 8½. 20351-4 Pa. $6.00

THE I CHING (THE BOOK OF CHANGES), translated by James Legge. Complete translation of basic text plus appendices by Confucius, and Chinese commentary of most penetrating divination manual ever prepared. Indispensable to study of early Oriental civilizations, to modern inquiring reader. 448pp. 5⅜ x 8½. 21062-6 Pa. $5.00

THE EGYPTIAN BOOK OF THE DEAD, E. A. Wallis Budge. Complete reproduction of Ani's papyrus, finest ever found. Full hieroglyphic text, interlinear transliteration, word for word translation, smooth translation. Basic work, for Egyptology, for modern study of psychic matters. Total of 533pp. 6½ x 9¼. (Available in U.S. only) 21866-X Pa. $5.95

THE GODS OF THE EGYPTIANS, E. A. Wallis Budge. Never excelled for richness, fullness: all gods, goddesses, demons, mythical figures of Ancient Egypt; their legends, rites, incarnations, variations, powers, etc. Many hieroglyphic texts cited. Over 225 illustrations, plus 6 color plates. Total of 988pp. 6⅛ x 9¼. (Available in U.S. only)
22055-9, 22056-7 Pa., Two-vol. set $16.00

THE STANDARD BOOK OF QUILT MAKING AND COLLECTING, Marguerite Ickis. Full information, full-sized patterns for making 46 traditional quilts, also 150 other patterns. Quilted cloths, lame, satin quilts, etc. 483 illustrations. 273pp. 6⅞ x 9⅝. 20582-7 Pa. $4.95

CORAL GARDENS AND THEIR MAGIC, Bronsilaw Malinowski. Classic study of the methods of tilling the soil and of agricultural rites in the Trobriand Islands of Melanesia. Author is one of the most important figures in the field of modern social anthropology. 143 illustrations. Indexes. Total of 911pp. of text. 5⅝ x 8¼. (Available in U.S. only)
23597-1 Pa. $12.95

THE PHILOSOPHY OF HISTORY, Georg W. Hegel. Great classic of Western thought develops concept that history is not chance but a rational process, the evolution of freedom. 457pp. 5⅜ x 8½. 20112-0 Pa. $4.50

LANGUAGE, TRUTH AND LOGIC, Alfred J. Ayer. Famous, clear introduction to Vienna, Cambridge schools of Logical Positivism. Role of philosophy, elimination of metaphysics, nature of analysis, etc. 160pp. 5⅜ x 8½. (Available in U.S. only) 20010-8 Pa. $2.00

A PREFACE TO LOGIC, Morris R. Cohen. Great City College teacher in renowned, easily followed exposition of formal logic, probability, values, logic and world order and similar topics; no previous background needed. 209pp. 5⅜ x 8½. 23517-3 Pa. $3.50

REASON AND NATURE, Morris R. Cohen. Brilliant analysis of reason and its multitudinous ramifications by charismatic teacher. Interdisciplinary, synthesizing work widely praised when it first appeared in 1931. Second (1953) edition. Indexes. 496pp. 5⅜ x 8½. 23633-1 Pa. $6.50

AN ESSAY CONCERNING HUMAN UNDERSTANDING, John Locke. The only complete edition of enormously important classic, with authoritative editorial material by A. C. Fraser. Total of 1176pp. 5⅜ x 8½. 20530-4, 20531-2 Pa., Two-vol. set $16.00

HANDBOOK OF MATHEMATICAL FUNCTIONS WITH FORMULAS, GRAPHS, AND MATHEMATICAL TABLES, edited by Milton Abramowitz and Irene A. Stegun. Vast compendium: 29 sets of tables, some to as high as 20 places. 1,046pp. 8 x 10½. 61272-4 Pa. $14.95

MATHEMATICS FOR THE PHYSICAL SCIENCES, Herbert S. Wilf. Highly acclaimed work offers clear presentations of vector spaces and matrices, orthogonal functions, roots of polynomial equations, conformal mapping, calculus of variations, etc. Knowledge of theory of functions of real and complex variables is assumed. Exercises and solutions. Index. 284pp. 5⅝ x 8¼. 63635-6 Pa. $5.00

THE PRINCIPLE OF RELATIVITY, Albert Einstein et al. Eleven most important original papers on special and general theories. Seven by Einstein, two by Lorentz, one each by Minkowski and Weyl. All translated, unabridged. 216pp. 5⅜ x 8½. 60081-5 Pa. $3.50

THERMODYNAMICS, Enrico Fermi. A classic of modern science. Clear, organized treatment of systems, first and second laws, entropy, thermodynamic potentials, gaseous reactions, dilute solutions, entropy constant. No math beyond calculus required. Problems. 160pp. 5⅜ x 8½. 60361-X Pa. $3.00

ELEMENTARY MECHANICS OF FLUIDS, Hunter Rouse. Classic undergraduate text widely considered to be far better than many later books. Ranges from fluid velocity and acceleration to role of compressibility in fluid motion. Numerous examples, questions, problems. 224 illustrations. 376pp. 5⅝ x 8¼. 63699-2 Pa. $5.00

THE COMPLETE BOOK OF DOLL MAKING AND COLLECTING, Catherine Christopher. Instructions, patterns for dozens of dolls, from rag doll on up to elaborate, historically accurate figures. Mould faces, sew clothing, make doll houses, etc. Also collecting information. Many illustrations. 288pp. 6 x 9. 22066-4 Pa. $4.50

THE DAGUERREOTYPE IN AMERICA, Beaumont Newhall. Wonderful portraits, 1850's townscapes, landscapes; full text plus 104 photographs. The basic book. Enlarged 1976 edition. 272pp. 8¼ x 11¼. 23322-7 Pa. $7.95

CRAFTSMAN HOMES, Gustav Stickley. 296 architectural drawings, floor plans, and photographs illustrate 40 different kinds of "Mission-style" homes from The Craftsman (1901-16), voice of American style of simplicity and organic harmony. Thorough coverage of Craftsman idea in text and picture, now collector's item. 224pp. 8⅛ x 11. 23791-5 Pa. $6.00

PEWTER-WORKING: INSTRUCTIONS AND PROJECTS, Burl N. Osborn. & Gordon O. Wilber. Introduction to pewter-working for amateur craftsman. History and characteristics of pewter; tools, materials, step-by-step instructions. Photos, line drawings, diagrams. Total of 160pp. 7⅞ x 10¾. 23786-9 Pa. $3.50

THE GREAT CHICAGO FIRE, edited by David Lowe. 10 dramatic, eyewitness accounts of the 1871 disaster, including one of the aftermath and rebuilding, plus 70 contemporary photographs and illustrations of the ruins—courthouse, Palmer House, Great Central Depot, etc. Introduction by David Lowe. 87pp. 8¼ x 11. 23771-0 Pa. $4.00

SILHOUETTES: A PICTORIAL ARCHIVE OF VARIED ILLUSTRATIONS, edited by Carol Belanger Grafton. Over 600 silhouettes from the 18th to 20th centuries include profiles and full figures of men and women, children, birds and animals, groups and scenes, nature, ships, an alphabet. Dozens of uses for commercial artists and craftspeople. 144pp. 8⅜ x 11¼. 23781-8 Pa. $4.50

ANIMALS: 1,419 COPYRIGHT-FREE ILLUSTRATIONS OF MAMMALS, BIRDS, FISH, INSECTS, ETC., edited by Jim Harter. Clear wood engravings present, in extremely lifelike poses, over 1,000 species of animals. One of the most extensive copyright-free pictorial sourcebooks of its kind. Captions. Index. 284pp. 9 x 12. 23766-4 Pa. $8.95

INDIAN DESIGNS FROM ANCIENT ECUADOR, Frederick W. Shaffer. 282 original designs by pre-Columbian Indians of Ecuador (500-1500 A.D.). Designs include people, mammals, birds, reptiles, fish, plants, heads, geometric designs. Use as is or alter for advertising, textiles, leathercraft, etc. Introduction. 95pp. 8¾ x 11¼. 23764-8 Pa. $3.50

SZIGETI ON THE VIOLIN, Joseph Szigeti. Genial, loosely structured tour by premier violinist, featuring a pleasant mixture of reminiscenes, insights into great music and musicians, innumerable tips for practicing violinists. 385 musical passages. 256pp. 5⅝ x 8¼. 23763-X Pa. $4.00

TONE POEMS, SERIES II: TILL EULENSPIEGELS LUSTIGE STREICHE, ALSO SPRACH ZARATHUSTRA, AND EIN HELDEN-LEBEN, Richard Strauss. Three important orchestral works, including very popular *Till Eulenspiegel's Marry Pranks,* reproduced in full score from original editions. Study score. 315pp. 9⅜ x 12¼. (Available in U.S. only) 23755-9 Pa. $8.95

TONE POEMS, SERIES I: DON JUAN, TOD UND VERKLARUNG AND DON QUIXOTE, Richard Strauss. Three of the most often performed and recorded works in entire orchestral repertoire, reproduced in full score from original editions. Study score. 286pp. 9⅜ x 12¼. (Available in U.S. only) 23754-0 Pa. $7.50

11 LATE STRING QUARTETS, Franz Joseph Haydn. The form which Haydn defined and "brought to perfection." *(Grove's).* 11 string quartets in complete score, his last and his best. The first in a projected series of the complete Haydn string quartets. Reliable modern Eulenberg edition, otherwise difficult to obtain. 320pp. 8⅜ x 11¼. (Available in U.S. only) 23753-2 Pa. $7.50

FOURTH, FIFTH AND SIXTH SYMPHONIES IN FULL SCORE, Peter Ilyitch Tchaikovsky. Complete orchestral scores of Symphony No. 4 in F Minor, Op. 36; Symphony No. 5 in E Minor, Op. 64; Symphony No. 6 in B Minor, "Pathetique," Op. 74. Bretikopf & Hartel eds. Study score. 480pp. 9⅜ x 12¼. 23861-X Pa. $10.95

THE MARRIAGE OF FIGARO: COMPLETE SCORE, Wolfgang A. Mozart. Finest comic opera ever written. Full score, not to be confused with piano renderings. Peters edition. Study score. 448pp. 9⅜ x 12¼. (Available in U.S. only) 23751-6 Pa. $11.95

"IMAGE" ON THE ART AND EVOLUTION OF THE FILM, edited by Marshall Deutelbaum. Pioneering book brings together for first time 38 groundbreaking articles on early silent films from *Image* and 263 illustrations newly shot from rare prints in the collection of the International Museum of Photography. A landmark work. Index. 256pp. 8¼ x 11. 23777-X Pa. $8.95

AROUND-THE-WORLD COOKY BOOK, Lois Lintner Sumption and Marguerite Lintner Ashbrook. 373 cooky and frosting recipes from 28 countries (America, Austria, China, Russia, Italy, etc.) include Viennese kisses, rice wafers, London strips, lady fingers, hony, sugar spice, maple cookies, etc. Clear instructions. All tested. 38 drawings. 182pp. 5⅜ x 8. 23802-4 Pa. $2.50

THE ART NOUVEAU STYLE, edited by Roberta Waddell. 579 rare photographs, not available elsewhere, of works in jewelry, metalwork, glass, ceramics, textiles, architecture and furniture by 175 artists—Mucha, Seguy, Lalique, Tiffany, Gaudin, Hohlwein, Saarinen, and many others. 288pp. 8⅜ x 11¼. 23515-7 Pa. $6.95

THE AMERICAN SENATOR, Anthony Trollope. Little known, long unavailable Trollope novel on a grand scale. Here are humorous comment on American vs. English culture, and stunning portrayal of a heroine/villainess. Superb evocation of Victorian village life. 561pp. 5⅜ x 8½.
23801-6 Pa. $6.00

WAS IT MURDER? James Hilton. The author of *Lost Horizon* and *Goodbye, Mr. Chips* wrote one detective novel (under a pen-name) which was quickly forgotten and virtually lost, even at the height of Hilton's fame. This edition brings it back—a finely crafted public school puzzle resplendent with Hilton's stylish atmosphere. A thoroughly English thriller by the creator of Shangri-la. 252pp. 5⅜ x 8. (Available in U.S. only)
23774-5 Pa. $3.00

CENTRAL PARK: A PHOTOGRAPHIC GUIDE, Victor Laredo and Henry Hope Reed. 121 superb photographs show dramatic views of Central Park: Bethesda Fountain, Cleopatra's Needle, Sheep Meadow, the Blockhouse, plus people engaged in many park activities: ice skating, bike riding, etc. Captions by former Curator of Central Park, Henry Hope Reed, provide historical view, changes, etc. Also photos of N.Y. landmarks on park's periphery. 96pp. 8½ x 11. 23750-8 Pa. $4.50

NANTUCKET IN THE NINETEENTH CENTURY, Clay Lancaster. 180 rare photographs, stereographs, maps, drawings and floor plans recreate unique American island society. Authentic scenes of shipwreck, lighthouses, streets, homes are arranged in geographic sequence to provide walking-tour guide to old Nantucket existing today. Introduction, captions. 160pp. 8⅞ x 11¾. 23747-8 Pa. $6.95

STONE AND MAN: A PHOTOGRAPHIC EXPLORATION, Andreas Feininger. 106 photographs by *Life* photographer Feininger portray man's deep passion for stone through the ages. Stonehenge-like megaliths, fortified towns, sculpted marble and crumbling tenements show textures, beauties, fascination. 128pp. 9¼ x 10¾. 23756-7 Pa. $5.95

CIRCLES, A MATHEMATICAL VIEW, D. Pedoe. Fundamental aspects of college geometry, non-Euclidean geometry, and other branches of mathematics: representing circle by point. Poincare model, isoperimetric property, etc. Stimulating recreational reading. 66 figures. 96pp. 5⅝ x 8¼.
63698-4 Pa. $2.75

THE DISCOVERY OF NEPTUNE, Morton Grosser. Dramatic scientific history of the investigations leading up to the actual discovery of the eighth planet of our solar system. Lucid, well-researched book by well-known historian of science. 172pp. 5⅜ x 8½. 23726-5 Pa. $3.50

SECOND PIATIGORSKY CUP, edited by Isaac Kashdan. One of the greatest tournament books ever produced in the English language. All 90 games of the 1966 tournament, annotated by players, most annotated by both players. Features Petrosian, Spassky, Fischer, Larsen, six others. 228pp. 5⅜ x 8½.   23572-6 Pa. $3.50

ENCYCLOPEDIA OF CARD TRICKS, revised and edited by Jean Hugard. How to perform over 600 card tricks, devised by the world's greatest magicians: impromptus, spelling tricks, key cards, using special packs, much, much more. Additional chapter on card technique. 66 illustrations. 402pp. 5⅜ x 8½. (Available in U.S. only)   21252-1 Pa. $4.95

MAGIC: STAGE ILLUSIONS, SPECIAL EFFECTS AND TRICK PHO-TOGRAPHY, Albert A. Hopkins, Henry R. Evans. One of the great classics; fullest, most authorative explanation of vanishing lady, levitations, scores of other great stage effects. Also small magic, automata, stunts. 446 illus-trations. 556pp. 5⅜ x 8½.   23344-8 Pa. $6.95

THE SECRETS OF HOUDINI, J. C. Cannell. Classic study of Houdini's incredible magic, exposing closely-kept professional secrets and revealing, in general terms, the whole art of stage magic. 67 illustrations. 279pp. 5⅜ x 8½.   22913-0 Pa. $4.00

HOFFMANN'S MODERN MAGIC, Professor Hoffmann. One of the best, and best-known, magicians' manuals of the past century. Hundreds of tricks from card tricks and simple sleight of hand to elaborate illusions involving construction of complicated machinery. 332 illustrations. 563pp. 5⅜ x 8½.   23623-4 Pa. $6.00

MADAME PRUNIER'S FISH COOKERY BOOK, Mme. S. B. Prunier. More than 1000 recipes from world famous Prunier's of Paris and London, specially adapted here for American kitchen. Grilled tournedos with anchovy butter, Lobster a la Bordelaise, Prunier's prized desserts, more. Glossary. 340pp. 5⅜ x 8½. (Available in U.S. only)   22679-4 Pa. $3.00

FRENCH COUNTRY COOKING FOR AMERICANS, Louis Diat. 500 easy-to-make, authentic provincial recipes compiled by former head chef at New York's Fitz-Carlton Hotel: onion soup, lamb stew, potato pie, more. 309pp. 5⅜ x 8½.   23665-X Pa. $3.95

SAUCES, FRENCH AND FAMOUS, Louis Diat. Complete book gives over 200 specific recipes: bechamel, Bordelaise, hollandaise, Cumberland, apri-cot, etc. Author was one of this century's finest chefs, originator of vichyssoise and many other dishes. Index. 156pp. 5⅜ x 8.
23663-3 Pa. $2.75

TOLL HOUSE TRIED AND TRUE RECIPES, Ruth Graves Wakefield. Authentic recipes from the famous Mass. restaurant: popovers, veal and ham loaf, Toll House baked beans, chocolate cake crumb pudding, much more. Many helpful hints. Nearly 700 recipes. Index. 376pp. 5⅜ x 8½.
23560-2 Pa. $4.50

"OSCAR" OF THE WALDORF'S COOKBOOK, Oscar Tschirky. Famous American chef reveals 3455 recipes that made Waldorf great; cream of French, German, American cooking, in all categories. Full instructions, easy home use. 1896 edition. 907pp. 6⅝ x 9⅜.   20790-0 Clothbd. $15.00

COOKING WITH BEER, Carole Fahy. Beer has as superb an effect on food as wine, and at fraction of cost. Over 250 recipes for appetizers, soups, main dishes, desserts, breads, etc. Index. 144pp. 5⅜ x 8½. (Available in U.S. only)   23661-7 Pa. $2.50

STEWS AND RAGOUTS, Kay Shaw Nelson. This international cookbook offers wide range of 108 recipes perfect for everyday, special occasions, meals-in-themselves, main dishes. Economical, nutritious, easy-to-prepare: goulash, Irish stew, boeuf bourguignon, etc. Index. 134pp. 5⅜ x 8½.
23662-5 Pa. $2.50

DELICIOUS MAIN COURSE DISHES, Marian Tracy. Main courses are the most important part of any meal. These 200 nutritious, economical recipes from around the world make every meal a delight. "I . . . have found it so useful in my own household,"—N.Y. Times. Index. 219pp. 5⅜ x 8½.   23664-1 Pa. $3.00

FIVE ACRES AND INDEPENDENCE, Maurice G. Kains. Great back-to-the-land classic explains basics of self-sufficient farming: economics, plants, crops, animals, orchards, soils, land selection, host of other necessary things. Do not confuse with skimpy faddist literature; Kains was one of America's greatest agriculturalists. 95 illustrations. 397pp. 5⅜ x 8½.
20974-1 Pa. $3.95

A PRACTICAL GUIDE FOR THE BEGINNING FARMER, Herbert Jacobs. Basic, extremely useful first book for anyone thinking about moving to the country and starting a farm. Simpler than Kains, with greater emphasis on country living in general. 246pp. 5⅜ x 8½.
23675-7 Pa. $3.50

PAPERMAKING, Dard Hunter. Definitive book on the subject by the foremost authority in the field. Chapters dealing with every aspect of history of craft in every part of the world. Over 320 illustrations. 2nd, revised and enlarged (1947) edition. 672pp. 5⅜ x 8½.   23619-6 Pa. $7.95

THE ART DECO STYLE, edited by Theodore Menten. Furniture, jewelry, metalwork, ceramics, fabrics, lighting fixtures, interior decors, exteriors, graphics from pure French sources. Best sampling around. Over 400 photographs. 183pp. 8⅜ x 11¼.   22824-X Pa. $6.00

ACKERMANN'S COSTUME PLATES, Rudolph Ackermann. Selection of 96 plates from the Repository of Arts, best published source of costume for English fashion during the early 19th century. 12 plates also in color. Captions, glossary and introduction by editor Stella Blum. Total of 120pp. 8⅜ x 11¼.   23690-0 Pa. $4.50

AMERICAN BIRD ENGRAVINGS, Alexander Wilson et al. All 76 plates. from Wilson's *American Ornithology* (1808-14), most important ornithological work before Audubon, plus 27 plates from the supplement (1825-33) by Charles Bonaparte. Over 250 birds portrayed. 8 plates also reproduced in full color. 111pp. 9⅜ x 12½.   23195-X Pa. $6.00

CRUICKSHANK'S PHOTOGRAPHS OF BIRDS OF AMERICA, Allan D. Cruickshank. Great ornithologist, photographer presents 177 closeups, groupings, panoramas, flightings, etc., of about 150 different birds. Expanded *Wings in the Wilderness*. Introduction by Helen G. Cruickshank. 191pp. 8¼ x 11.   23497-5 Pa. $6.00

AMERICAN WILDLIFE AND PLANTS, A. C. Martin, et al. Describes food habits of more than 1000 species of mammals, birds, fish. Special treatment of important food plants. Over 300 illustrations. 500pp. 5⅜ x 8½.
20793-5 Pa. $4.95

THE PEOPLE CALLED SHAKERS, Edward D. Andrews. Lifetime of research, definitive study of Shakers: origins, beliefs, practices, dances, social organization, furniture and crafts, impact on 19th-century USA, present heritage. Indispensable to student of American history, collector. 33 illustrations. 351pp. 5⅜ x 8½.   21081-2 Pa. $4.50

OLD NEW YORK IN EARLY PHOTOGRAPHS, Mary Black. New York City as it was in 1853-1901, through 196 wonderful photographs from N.-Y. Historical Society. Great Blizzard, Lincoln's funeral procession, great buildings. 228pp. 9 x 12.   22907-6 Pa. $8.95

MR. LINCOLN'S CAMERA MAN: MATHEW BRADY, Roy Meredith. Over 300 Brady photos reproduced directly from original negatives, photos. Jackson, Webster, Grant, Lee, Carnegie, Barnum; Lincoln; Battle Smoke, Death of Rebel Sniper, Atlanta Just After Capture. Lively commentary. 368pp. 8⅜ x 11¼.   23021-X Pa. $8.95

TRAVELS OF WILLIAM BARTRAM, William Bartram. From 1773-8, Bartram explored Northern Florida, Georgia, Carolinas, and reported on wild life, plants, Indians, early settlers. Basic account for period, entertaining reading. Edited by Mark Van Doren. 13 illustrations. 141pp. 5⅜ x 8½.   20013-2 Pa. $5.00

THE GENTLEMAN AND CABINET MAKER'S DIRECTOR, Thomas Chippendale. Full reprint, 1762 style book, most influential of all time; chairs, tables, sofas, mirrors, cabinets, etc. 200 plates, plus 24 photographs of surviving pieces. 249pp. 9⅞ x 12¾.   21601-2 Pa. $7.95

AMERICAN CARRIAGES, SLEIGHS, SULKIES AND CARTS, edited by Don H. Berkebile. 168 Victorian illustrations from catalogues, trade journals, fully captioned. Useful for artists. Author is Assoc. Curator, Div. of Transportation of Smithsonian Institution. 168pp. 8½ x 9½.
23328-6 Pa. $5.00

YUCATAN BEFORE AND AFTER THE CONQUEST, Diego de Landa. First English translation of basic book in Maya studies, the only significant account of Yucatan written in the early post-Conquest era. Translated by distinguished Maya scholar William Gates. Appendices, introduction, 4 maps and over 120 illustrations added by translator. 162pp. 5⅜ x 8½.
23622-6 Pa. $3.00

THE MALAY ARCHIPELAGO, Alfred R. Wallace. Spirited travel account by one of founders of modern biology. Touches on zoology, botany, ethnography, geography, and geology. 62 illustrations, maps. 515pp. 5⅜ x 8½.
20187-2 Pa. $6.95

THE DISCOVERY OF THE TOMB OF TUTANKHAMEN, Howard Carter, A. C. Mace. Accompany Carter in the thrill of discovery, as ruined passage suddenly reveals unique, untouched, fabulously rich tomb. Fascinating account, with 106 illustrations. New introduction by J. M. White. Total of 382pp. 5⅜ x 8½. (Available in U.S. only)   23500-9 Pa. $4.00

THE WORLD'S GREATEST SPEECHES, edited by Lewis Copeland and Lawrence W. Lamm. Vast collection of 278 speeches from Greeks up to present. Powerful and effective models; unique look at history. Revised to 1970. Indices. 842pp. 5⅜ x 8½.   20468-5 Pa. $8.95

THE 100 GREATEST ADVERTISEMENTS, Julian Watkins. The priceless ingredient; His master's voice; 99 44/100% pure; over 100 others. How they were written, their impact, etc. Remarkable record. 130 illustrations. 233pp. 7⅞ x 10 3/5.   20540-1 Pa. $5.95

CRUICKSHANK PRINTS FOR HAND COLORING, George Cruickshank. 18 illustrations, one side of a page, on fine-quality paper suitable for watercolors. Caricatures of people in society (c. 1820) full of trenchant wit. Very large format. 32pp. 11 x 16.   23684-6 Pa. $5.00

THIRTY-TWO COLOR POSTCARDS OF TWENTIETH-CENTURY AMERICAN ART, Whitney Museum of American Art. Reproduced in full color in postcard form are 31 art works and one shot of the museum. Calder, Hopper, Rauschenberg, others. Detachable. 16pp. 8¼ x 11.
23629-3 Pa. $3.00

MUSIC OF THE SPHERES: THE MATERIAL UNIVERSE FROM ATOM TO QUASAR SIMPLY EXPLAINED, Guy Murchie. Planets, stars, geology, atoms, radiation, relativity, quantum theory, light, antimatter, similar topics. 319 figures. 664pp. 5⅜ x 8½.
21809-0, 21810-4 Pa., Two-vol. set $11.00

EINSTEIN'S THEORY OF RELATIVITY, Max Born. Finest semi-technical account; covers Einstein, Lorentz, Minkowski, and others, with much detail, much explanation of ideas and math not readily available elsewhere on this level. For student, non-specialist. 376pp. 5⅜ x 8½.
60769-0 Pa. $4.50

THE EARLY WORK OF AUBREY BEARDSLEY, Aubrey Beardsley. 157 plates, 2 in color: *Manon Lescaut, Madame Bovary, Morte Darthur, Salome,* other. Introduction by H. Marillier. 182pp. 8⅛ x 11. 21816-3 Pa. $4.50

THE LATER WORK OF AUBREY BEARDSLEY, Aubrey Beardsley. Exotic masterpieces of full maturity: *Venus and Tannhauser, Lysistrata, Rape of the Lock, Volpone,* Savoy material, etc. 174 plates, 2 in color. 186pp. 8⅛ x 11. 21817-1 Pa. $5.95

THOMAS NAST'S CHRISTMAS DRAWINGS, Thomas Nast. Almost all Christmas drawings by creator of image of Santa Claus as we know it, and one of America's foremost illustrators and political cartoonists. 66 illustrations. 3 illustrations in color on covers. 96pp. 8⅜ x 11¼. 23660-9 Pa. $3.50

THE DORÉ ILLUSTRATIONS FOR DANTE'S DIVINE COMEDY, Gustave Doré. All 135 plates from Inferno, Purgatory, Paradise; fantastic tortures, infernal landscapes, celestial wonders. Each plate with appropriate (translated) verses. 141pp. 9 x 12. 23231-X Pa. $4.50

DORÉ'S ILLUSTRATIONS FOR RABELAIS, Gustave Doré. 252 striking illustrations of *Gargantua and Pantagruel* books by foremost 19th-century illustrator. Including 60 plates, 192 delightful smaller illustrations. 153pp. 9 x 12. 23656-0 Pa. $5.00

LONDON: A PILGRIMAGE, Gustave Doré, Blanchard Jerrold. Squalor, riches, misery, beauty of mid-Victorian metropolis; 55 wonderful plates, 125 other illustrations, full social, cultural text by Jerrold. 191pp. of text. 9⅜ x 12¼. 22306-X Pa. $7.00

THE RIME OF THE ANCIENT MARINER, Gustave Doré, S. T. Coleridge. Dore's finest work, 34 plates capture moods, subtleties of poem. Full text. Introduction by Millicent Rose. 77pp. 9¼ x 12. 22305-1 Pa. $3.50

THE DORE BIBLE ILLUSTRATIONS, Gustave Doré. All wonderful, detailed plates: Adam and Eve, Flood, Babylon, Life of Jesus, etc. Brief King James text with each plate. Introduction by Millicent Rose. 241 plates. 241pp. 9 x 12. 23004-X Pa. $6.00

THE COMPLETE ENGRAVINGS, ETCHINGS AND DRYPOINTS OF ALBRECHT DURER. "Knight, Death and Devil"; "Melencolia," and more—all Dürer's known works in all three media, including 6 works formerly attributed to him. 120 plates. 235pp. 8⅜ x 11¼. 22851-7 Pa. $6.50

MECHANICK EXERCISES ON THE WHOLE ART OF PRINTING, Joseph Moxon. First complete book (1683-4) ever written about typography, a compendium of everything known about printing at the latter part of 17th century. Reprint of 2nd (1962) Oxford Univ. Press edition. 74 illustrations. Total of 550pp. 6⅛ x 9¼. 23617-X Pa. $7.95

THE COMPLETE WOODCUTS OF ALBRECHT DURER, edited by Dr. W. Kurth. 346 in all: "Old Testament," "St. Jerome," "Passion," "Life of Virgin," Apocalypse," many others. Introduction by Campbell Dodgson. 285pp. 8½ x 12¼. 21097-9 Pa. $7.50

DRAWINGS OF ALBRECHT DURER, edited by Heinrich Wolfflin. 81 plates show development from youth to full style. Many favorites; many new. Introduction by Alfred Werner. 96pp. 8⅛ x 11. 22352-3 Pa. $5.00

THE HUMAN FIGURE, Albrecht Dürer. Experiments in various techniques—stereometric, progressive proportional, and others. Also life studies that rank among finest ever done. Complete reprinting of *Dresden Sketchbook*. 170 plates. 355pp. 8⅜ x 11¼. 21042-1 Pa. $7.95

OF THE JUST SHAPING OF LETTERS, Albrecht Dürer. Renaissance artist explains design of Roman majuscules by geometry, also Gothic lower and capitals. Grolier Club edition. 43pp. 7⅞ x 10¾ 21306-4 Pa. $3.00

TEN BOOKS ON ARCHITECTURE, Vitruvius. The most important book ever written on architecture. Early Roman aesthetics, technology, classical orders, site selection, all other aspects. Stands behind everything since. Morgan translation. 331pp. 5⅜ x 8½. 20645-9 Pa. $4.50

THE FOUR BOOKS OF ARCHITECTURE, Andrea Palladio. 16th-century classic responsible for Palladian movement and style. Covers classical architectural remains, Renaissance revivals, classical orders, etc. 1738 Ware English edition. Introduction by A. Placzek. 216 plates. 110pp. of text. 9½ x 12¾. 21308-0 Pa. $10.00

HORIZONS, Norman Bel Geddes. Great industrialist stage designer, "father of streamlining," on application of aesthetics to transportation, amusement, architecture, etc. 1932 prophetic account; function, theory, specific projects. 222 illustrations. 312pp. 7⅞ x 10¾. 23514-9 Pa. $6.95

FRANK LLOYD WRIGHT'S FALLINGWATER, Donald Hoffmann. Full, illustrated story of conception and building of Wright's masterwork at Bear Run, Pa. 100 photographs of site, construction, and details of completed structure. 112pp. 9¼ x 10. 23671-4 Pa. $5.50

THE ELEMENTS OF DRAWING, John Ruskin. Timeless classic by great Viltorian; starts with basic ideas, works through more difficult. Many practical exercises. 48 illustrations. Introduction by Lawrence Campbell. 228pp. 5⅜ x 8½. 22730-8 Pa. $3.75

GIST OF ART, John Sloan. Greatest modern American teacher, Art Students League, offers innumerable hints, instructions, guided comments to help you in painting. Not a formal course. 46 illustrations. Introduction by Helen Sloan. 200pp. 5⅜ x 8½. 23435-5 Pa. $4.00

THE ANATOMY OF THE HORSE, George Stubbs. Often considered the great masterpiece of animal anatomy. Full reproduction of 1766 edition, plus prospectus; original text and modernized text. 36 plates. Introduction by Eleanor Garvey. 121pp. 11 x 14¾. 23402-9 Pa. $6.00

BRIDGMAN'S LIFE DRAWING, George B. Bridgman. More than 500 illustrative drawings and text teach you to abstract the body into its major masses, use light and shade, proportion; as well as specific areas of anatomy, of which Bridgman is master. 192pp. 6½ x 9¼. (Available in U.S. only) 22710-3 Pa. $3.50

ART NOUVEAU DESIGNS IN COLOR, Alphonse Mucha, Maurice Verneuil, Georges Auriol. Full-color reproduction of *Combinaisons ornementales* (c. 1900) by Art Nouveau masters. Floral, animal, geometric, interlacings, swashes—borders, frames, spots—all incredibly beautiful. 60 plates, hundreds of designs. 9⅜ x 8-1/16. 22885-1 Pa. $4.00

FULL-COLOR FLORAL DESIGNS IN THE ART NOUVEAU STYLE, E. A. Seguy. 166 motifs, on 40 plates, from *Les fleurs et leurs applications decoratives* (1902): borders, circular designs, repeats, allovers, "spots." All in authentic Art Nouveau colors. 48pp. 9⅜ x 12¼. 23439-8 Pa. $5.00

A DIDEROT PICTORIAL ENCYCLOPEDIA OF TRADES AND IN-DUSTRY, edited by Charles C. Gillispie. 485 most interesting plates from the great French Encyclopedia of the 18th century show hundreds of working figures, artifacts, process, land and cityscapes; glassmaking, papermaking, metal extraction, construction, weaving, making furniture, clothing, wigs, dozens of other activities. Plates fully explained. 920pp. 9 x 12. 22284-5, 22285-3 Clothbd., Two-vol. set $40.00

HANDBOOK OF EARLY ADVERTISING ART, Clarence P. Hornung. Largest collection of copyright-free early and antique advertising art ever compiled. Over 6,000 illustrations, from Franklin's time to the 1890's for special effects, novelty. Valuable source, almost inexhaustible.
Pictorial Volume. Agriculture, the zodiac, animals, autos, birds, Christmas, fire engines, flowers, trees, musical instruments, ships, games and sports, much more. Arranged by subject matter and use. 237 plates. 288pp. 9 x 12. 20122-8 Clothbd. $14..50

Typographical Volume. Roman and Gothic faces ranging from 10 point to 300 point, "Barnum," German and Old English faces, script, logotypes, scrolls and flourishes, 1115 ornamental initials, 67 complete alphabets, more. 310 plates. 320pp. 9 x 12. 20123-6 Clothbd. $15.00

CALLIGRAPHY (CALLIGRAPHIA LATINA), J. G. Schwandner. High point of 18th-century ornamental calligraphy. Very ornate initials, scrolls, borders, cherubs, birds, lettered examples. 172pp. 9 x 13. 20475-8 Pa. $7.00

THE DEPRESSION YEARS AS PHOTOGRAPHED BY ARTHUR ROTH-STEIN, Arthur Rothstein. First collection devoted entirely to the work of outstanding 1930s photographer: famous dust storm photo, ragged children, unemployed, etc. 120 photographs. Captions. 119pp. 9¼ x 10¾.
23590-4 Pa. $5.00

CAMERA WORK: A PICTORIAL GUIDE, Alfred Stieglitz. All 559 illustrations and plates from the most important periodical in the history of art photography, Camera Work (1903-17). Presented four to a page, reduced in size but still clear, in strict chronological order, with complete captions. Three indexes. Glossary. Bibliography. 176pp. 8⅜ x 11¼.
23591-2 Pa. $6.95

ALVIN LANGDON COBURN, PHOTOGRAPHER, Alvin L. Coburn. Revealing autobiography by one of greatest photographers of 20th century gives insider's version of Photo-Secession, plus comments on his own work. 77 photographs by Coburn. Edited by Helmut and Alison Gernsheim. 160pp. 8⅛ x 11.
23685-4 Pa. $6.00

NEW YORK IN THE FORTIES, Andreas Feininger. 162 brilliant photographs by the well-known photographer, formerly with Life magazine, show commuters, shoppers, Times Square at night, Harlem nightclub, Lower East Side, etc. Introduction and full captions by John von Hartz. 181pp. 9¼ x 10¾.
23585-8 Pa. $6.95

GREAT NEWS PHOTOS AND THE STORIES BEHIND THEM, John Faber. Dramatic volume of 140 great news photos, 1855 through 1976, and revealing stories behind them, with both historical and technical information. Hindenburg disaster, shooting of Oswald, nomination of Jimmy Carter, etc. 160pp. 8¼ x 11.
23667-6 Pa. $5.00

THE ART OF THE CINEMATOGRAPHER, Leonard Maltin. Survey of American cinematography history and anecdotal interviews with 5 masters—Arthur Miller, Hal Mohr, Hal Rosson, Lucien Ballard, and Conrad Hall. Very large selection of behind-the-scenes production photos. 105 photographs. Filmographies. Index. Originally Behind the Camera. 144pp. 8¼ x 11.
23686-2 Pa. $5.00

DESIGNS FOR THE THREE-CORNERED HAT (LE TRICORNE), Pablo Picasso. 32 fabulously rare drawings—including 31 color illustrations of costumes and accessories—for 1919 production of famous ballet. Edited by Parmenia Migel, who has written new introduction. 48pp. 9⅜ x 12¼. (Available in U.S. only)
23709-5 Pa. $5.00

NOTES OF A FILM DIRECTOR, Sergei Eisenstein. Greatest Russian filmmaker explains montage, making of Alexander Nevsky, aesthetics; comments on self, associates, great rivals (Chaplin), similar material. 78 illustrations. 240pp. 5⅜ x 8½.
22392-2 Pa. $4.50

HOLLYWOOD GLAMOUR PORTRAITS, edited by John Kobal. 145 photos capture the stars from 1926-49, the high point in portrait photography. Gable, Harlow, Bogart, Bacall, Hedy Lamarr, Marlene Dietrich, Robert Montgomery, Marlon Brando, Veronica Lake; 94 stars in all. Full background on photographers, technical aspects, much more. Total of 160pp. 8⅜ x 11¼. 23352-9 Pa. $6.00

THE NEW YORK STAGE: FAMOUS PRODUCTIONS IN PHOTO-GRAPHS, edited by Stanley Appelbaum. 148 photographs from Museum of City of New York show 142 plays, 1883-1939. *Peter Pan, The Front Page, Dead End, Our Town,* O'Neill, hundreds of actors and actresses, etc. Full indexes. 154pp. 9½ x 10. 23241-7 Pa. $6.00

DIALOGUES CONCERNING TWO NEW SCIENCES, Galileo Galilei. Encompassing 30 years of experiment and thought, these dialogues deal with geometric demonstrations of fracture of solid bodies, cohesion, leverage, speed of light and sound, pendulums, falling bodies, accelerated motion, etc. 300pp. 5⅜ x 8½. 60099-8 Pa. $4.00

THE GREAT OPERA STARS IN HISTORIC PHOTOGRAPHS, edited by James Camner. 343 portraits from the 1850s to the 1940s: Tamburini, Mario, Caliapin, Jeritza, Melchior, Melba, Patti, Pinza, Schipa, Caruso, Farrar, Steber, Gobbi, and many more—270 performers in all. Index. 199pp. 8⅜ x 11¼. 23575-0 Pa. $7.50

J. S. BACH, Albert Schweitzer. Great full-length study of Bach, life, background to music, music, by foremost modern scholar. Ernest Newman translation. 650 musical examples. Total of 928pp. 5⅜ x 8½. (Available in U.S. only) 21631-4, 21632-2 Pa., Two-vol. set $11.00

COMPLETE PIANO SONATAS, Ludwig van Beethoven. All sonatas in the fine Schenker edition, with fingering, analytical material. One of best modern editions. Total of 615pp. 9 x 12. (Available in U.S. only) 23134-8, 23135-6 Pa., Two-vol. set $15.50

KEYBOARD MUSIC, J. S. Bach. Bach-Gesellschaft edition. For harpsichord, piano, other keyboard instruments. English Suites, French Suites, Six Partitas, Goldberg Variations, Two-Part Inventions, Three-Part Sinfonias. 312pp. 8⅛ x 11. (Available in U.S. only) 22360-4 Pa. $6.95

FOUR SYMPHONIES IN FULL SCORE, Franz Schubert. Schubert's four most popular symphonies: No. 4 in C Minor ("Tragic"); No. 5 in B-flat Major; No. 8 in B Minor ("Unfinished"); No. 9 in C Major ("Great"). Breitkopf & Hartel edition. Study score. 261pp. 9⅜ x 12¼. 23681-1 Pa. $6.50

THE AUTHENTIC GILBERT & SULLIVAN SONGBOOK, W. S. Gilbert, A. S. Sullivan. Largest selection available; 92 songs, uncut, original keys, in piano rendering approved by Sullivan. Favorites and lesser-known fine numbers. Edited with plot synopses by James Spero. 3 illustrations. 399pp. 9 x 12. 23482-7 Pa. $9.95

PRINCIPLES OF ORCHESTRATION, Nikolay Rimsky-Korsakov. Great classical orchestrator provides fundamentals of tonal resonance, progression of parts, voice and orchestra, tutti effects, much else in major document. 330pp. of musical excerpts. 489pp. 6½ x 9¼.   21266-1 Pa. $7.50

TRISTAN UND ISOLDE, Richard Wagner. Full orchestral score with complete instrumentation. Do not confuse with piano reduction. Commentary by Felix Mottl, great Wagnerian conductor and scholar. Study score. 655pp. 8⅛ x 11.   22915-7 Pa. $13.95

REQUIEM IN FULL SCORE, Giuseppe Verdi. Immensely popular with choral groups and music lovers. Republication of edition published by C. F. Peters, Leipzig, n. d. German frontmaker in English translation. Glossary. Text in Latin. Study score. 204pp. 9⅜ x 12¼.
23682-X Pa. $6.00

COMPLETE CHAMBER MUSIC FOR STRINGS, Felix Mendelssohn. All of Mendelssohn's chamber music: Octet, 2 Quintets, 6 Quartets, and Four Pieces for String Quartet. (Nothing with piano is included). Complete works edition (1874-7). Study score. 283 pp. 9⅜ x 12¼.
23679-X Pa. $7.50

POPULAR SONGS OF NINETEENTH-CENTURY AMERICA, edited by Richard Jackson. 64 most important songs: "Old Oaken Bucket," "Arkansas Traveler," "Yellow Rose of Texas," etc. Authentic original sheet music, full introduction and commentaries. 290pp. 9 x 12.   23270-0 Pa. $7.95

COLLECTED PIANO WORKS, Scott Joplin. Edited by Vera Brodsky Lawrence. Practically all of Joplin's piano works—rags, two-steps, marches, waltzes, etc., 51 works in all. Extensive introduction by Rudi Blesh. Total of 345pp. 9 x 12.   23106-2 Pa. $14.95

BASIC PRINCIPLES OF CLASSICAL BALLET, Agrippina Vaganova. Great Russian theoretician, teacher explains methods for teaching classical ballet; incorporates best from French, Italian, Russian schools. 118 illustrations. 175pp. 5⅜ x 8½.   22036-2 Pa. $2.50

CHINESE CHARACTERS, L. Wieger. Rich analysis of 2300 characters according to traditional systems into primitives. Historical-semantic analysis to phonetics (Classical Mandarin) and radicals. 820pp. 6⅛ x 9¼.
21321-8 Pa. $10.00

EGYPTIAN LANGUAGE: EASY LESSONS IN EGYPTIAN HIERO-GLYPHICS, E. A. Wallis Budge. Foremost Egyptologist offers Egyptian grammar, explanation of hieroglyphics, many reading texts, dictionary of symbols. 246pp. 5 x 7½. (Available in U.S. only)
21394-3 Clothbd. $7.50

AN ETYMOLOGICAL DICTIONARY OF MODERN ENGLISH, Ernest Weekley. Richest, fullest work, by foremost British lexicographer. Detailed word histories. Inexhaustible. Do not confuse this with Concise Etymological Dictionary, which is abridged. Total of 856pp. 6½ x 9¼.
21873-2, 21874-0 Pa., Two-vol. set $12.00

AMERICAN ANTIQUE FURNITURE, Edgar G. Miller, Jr. The basic coverage of all American furniture before 1840: chapters per item chronologically cover all types of furniture, with more than 2100 photos. Total of 1106pp. 7⅞ x 10¾. 21599-7, 21600-4 Pa., Two-vol. set $17.90

ILLUSTRATED GUIDE TO SHAKER FURNITURE, Robert Meader. Director, Shaker Museum, Old Chatham, presents up-to-date coverage of all furniture and appurtenances, with much on local styles not available elsewhere. 235 photos. 146pp. 9 x 12. 22819-3 Pa. $6.00

ORIENTAL RUGS, ANTIQUE AND MODERN, Walter A. Hawley. Persia, Turkey, Caucasus, Central Asia, China, other traditions. Best general survey of all aspects: styles and periods, manufacture, uses, symbols and their interpretation, and identification. 96 illustrations, 11 in color. 320pp. 6⅛ x 9¼. 22366-3 Pa. $6.95

CHINESE POTTERY AND PORCELAIN, R. L. Hobson. Detailed descriptions and analyses by former Keeper of the Department of Oriental Antiquities and Ethnography at the British Museum. Covers hundreds of pieces from primitive times to 1915. Still the standard text for most periods. 136 plates, 40 in full color. Total of 750pp. 5⅜ x 8½. 23253-0 Pa. $10.00

THE WARES OF THE MING DYNASTY, R. L. Hobson. Foremost scholar examines and illustrates many varieties of Ming (1368-1644). Famous blue and white, polychrome, lesser-known styles and shapes. 117 illustrations, 9 full color, of outstanding pieces. Total of 263pp. 6⅛ x 9¼. (Available in U.S. only) 23652-8 Pa. $6.00

Prices subject to change without notice.

Available at your book dealer or write for free catalogue to Dept. GI, Dover Publications, Inc., 180 Varick St., N.Y., N.Y. 10014. Dover publishes more than 175 books each year on science, elementary and advanced mathematics, biology, music, art, literary history, social sciences and other areas.